公式 TOEIC® Listening & Reading トレーニング

リスニング編

一般財団法人 国際ビジネスコミュニケーション協会

ETS TOEIC®
OFFICIAL TEST PREPARATION AND LEARNING

はじめに

本書『公式 TOEIC® Listening & Reading トレーニング 2　リスニング編』は、TOEIC® Listening & Reading Test のリスニングセクションに対応した教材です。

※ リーディングセクションには、『公式 TOEIC® Listening & Reading トレーニング 2　リーディング編』が対応しています。

本書は、リスニングセクションの学習に力を入れたい方々がより多くの問題を解くことができるよう、20 セクションに分けて合計 380 問を掲載しています。問題は全てテスト開発機関 ETS が実際のテストと同じプロセスで制作し、TOEIC® 公式スピーカーによる音声を使用しています。

本書を TOEIC® Listening & Reading Test のリスニングセクションの受験準備、そして皆さまの英語学習にお役立ていただけることを願っております。

2023 年 12 月
一般財団法人 国際ビジネスコミュニケーション協会

音声ダウンロードの手順

※ 株式会社 Globee が提供するサービス abceed への会員登録（無料）が必要です。

1. パソコンまたはスマートフォンで音声ダウンロード用サイトにアクセスします。
右の QR コードまたはブラウザから下記にアクセスしてください。
https://app.abceed.com/audio/iibc-officialprep

2. 表示されたページから、abceed の新規会員登録を行います。
すでに会員の方は、ログイン情報を入力して上記 1. のサイトにアクセスします。

3. 上記 1. のサイトにアクセス後、本書の表紙画像をクリックします。
クリックすると、教材詳細画面へ移動します。

4. スマートフォンの場合は、アプリ「abceed」の案内が出ますので、アプリからご利用ください。
パソコンの場合は、教材詳細画面の「音声」のアイコンからご利用ください。
※ 音声は何度でもダウンロード・再生ができます。

ダウンロードについてのお問い合わせは下記にご連絡ください。
E メール：support@globeejphelp.zendesk.com
（お問い合わせ窓口の営業日：祝日を除く月～金曜日）

目　次

本冊

■はじめに／音声ダウンロードの手順 …… 3
■ TOEIC® Listening & Reading Test について／TOEIC® L&R の問題形式 …… 5
■本書の使い方 …… 6
■ Part 1 ～ 4 の問題形式および Directions（指示文）とその訳 …… 8

Section 1 …… 11
Section 2 …… 15
Section 3 …… 19
Section 4 …… 23
Section 5 …… 27
Section 6 …… 31
Section 7 …… 35
Section 8 …… 39
Section 9 …… 43
Section 10 …… 47
Section 11 …… 51
Section 12 …… 55
Section 13 …… 59
Section 14 …… 63
Section 15 …… 67
Section 16 …… 71
Section 17 …… 75
Section 18 …… 79
Section 19 …… 83
Section 20 …… 87

※各セクションの正解・スクリプト・訳は別冊に掲載しています。

TOEIC® Listening & Reading Test について

TOEIC® Program は、日常生活やグローバルビジネスにおける活きた英語力を測定する世界共通のテストで、現在 4 種類のテストがあります。その 1 つである TOEIC® Listening & Reading Test（以下 TOEIC® L&R）は、「聞く」「読む」の 2 つの英語力を測定するためのテストです。

最大の特長は、テスト結果を合格・不合格ではなく、リスニングセクション 5 点～ 495 点、リーディングセクション 5 点～ 495 点、トータル 10 点～ 990 点のスコアで評価することです。そのスコア基準は常に一定であり、受験者の英語能力に変化がない限りスコアも一定に保たれます。これにより、受験者は正確に現在の英語能力を把握したり、目標とするスコアを設定したりすることができます。

※ 最新の情報については IIBC 公式サイト https://www.iibc-global.org をご参照ください。

TOEIC® L&R の問題形式

- リスニングセクション（約 45 分間・100 問）と、リーディングセクション（75 分間・100 問）から成り、約 2 時間で 200 問に解答します。途中、休憩はありません。
- テストは英文のみで構成されており、英文和訳や和文英訳といった設問はありません。
- マークシート方式の一斉客観テストです。

※ テスト中、問題用紙への書き込みは一切禁じられています。

リスニングセクション（約 45 分間）

パート	Name of Each Part	パート名	問題数
1	Photographs	写真描写問題	6
2	Question-Response	応答問題	25
3	Conversations	会話問題	39
4	Talks	説明文問題	30

リーディングセクション（75 分間）

※ 本書ではリーディングセクションの問題は掲載していません。

パート	Name of Each Part	パート名	問題数
5	Incomplete Sentences	短文穴埋め問題	30
6	Text Completion	長文穴埋め問題	16
7	・Single passages	1 つの文書	29
	・Multiple passages	複数の文書	25

本書の使い方

本書では、TOEIC® L&R リスニングセクション（Part 1～Part 4）の全380問をSection 1～Section 20の20のセクションに分けて学習します。

問題を解く

本冊 **問題**

8～9ページに各パートのDirections（指示文）を掲載しているので、まずこれらの指示文を確認してから、学習を始めましょう。

各セクションには、Part 1～Part 4の全パートの問題が19問【Part 1：1問／Part 2：6問／Part 3：6問（2会話）／Part 4：6問（2トーク）】掲載されています。1つのセクションの解答所要時間は約10分です。

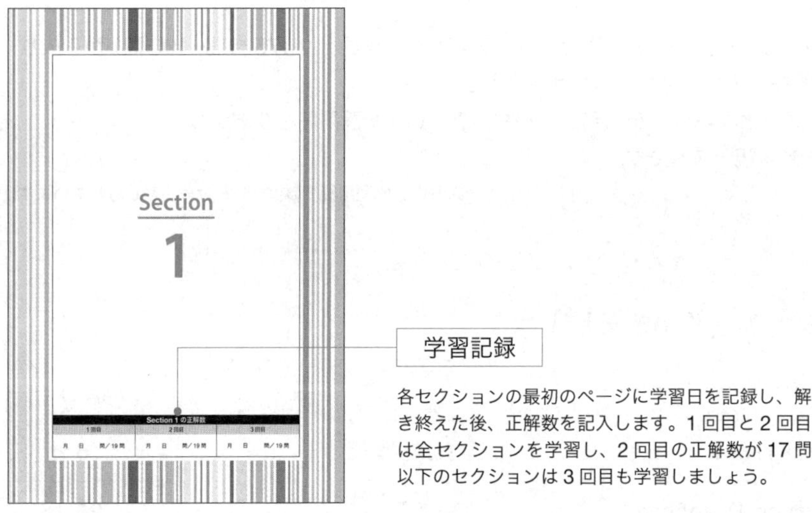

Section
1
Section 1 の正解数
1回目
2回目
3回目
月 日 問／19問
月 日 問／19問
月 日 問／19問
学習記録
各セクションの最初のページに学習日を記録し、解き終えた後、正解数を記入します。1回目と2回目は全セクションを学習し、2回目の正解数が17問以下のセクションは3回目も学習しましょう。

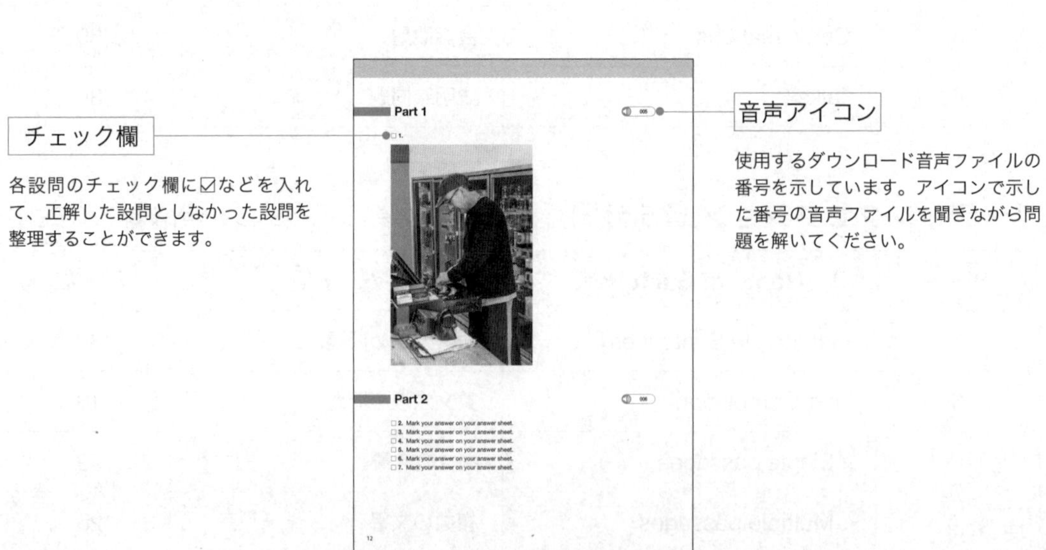

チェック欄
各設問のチェック欄に☑などを入れて、正解した設問としなかった設問を整理することができます。
Part 1
1.
Part 2
2. Mark your answer on your answer sheet.
3. Mark your answer on your answer sheet.
4. Mark your answer on your answer sheet.
5. Mark your answer on your answer sheet.
6. Mark your answer on your answer sheet.
7. Mark your answer on your answer sheet.
12
音声アイコン
使用するダウンロード音声ファイルの番号を示しています。アイコンで示した番号の音声ファイルを聞きながら問題を解いてください。

正解と内容を確認する

別冊　正解／スクリプト／訳

各セクションの問題に解答後、別冊で正解を確認しましょう。間違えた設問は本冊のチェック欄に自分なりの方法で印を付けましょう。その後スクリプトで英文を確認したら、音声を再度聞いてどのように聞こえるかをきちんと確かめ、正解できなかった理由を考えましょう。また音読やリピーティングで復習することもお勧めです。

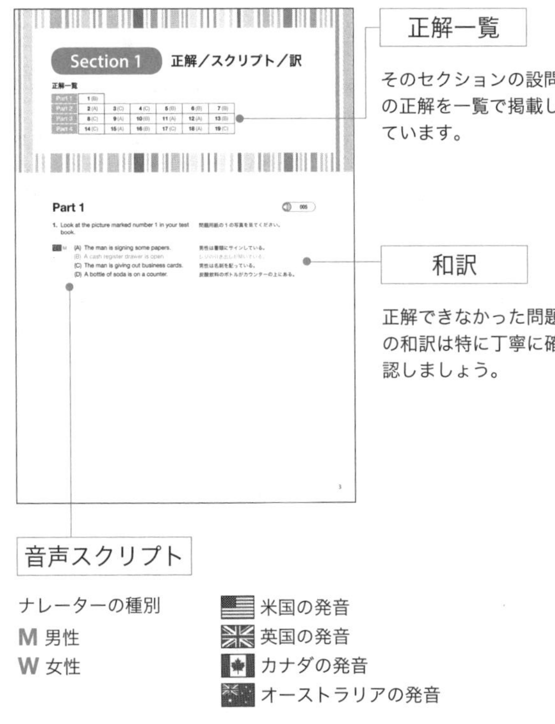

1セクションの進め方の例

※1日に1セクションを行えば、20日間で一通り解き終えることができます。

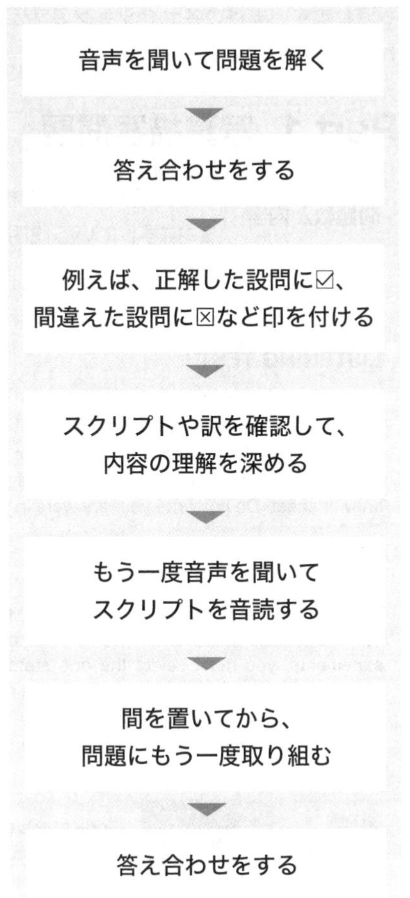

音声を聞いて問題を解く
答え合わせをする
例えば、正解した設問に☑、
間違えた設問に☒など印を付ける
スクリプトや訳を確認して、
内容の理解を深める
もう一度音声を聞いて
スクリプトを音読する
間を置いてから、
問題にもう一度取り組む
答え合わせをする

Section 20まで解き終えたら、もう一度Section 1から問題を解いてみましょう。
1回解答しただけで終わらせず、何度も繰り返して学習することが、英語力向上のために効果的です。

本番のTOEIC® L&Rを受験する前に

本書で繰り返し学習を終えた後は、テスト本番の受験に向けて感覚を養うために、『公式TOEIC® Listening & Reading問題集』シリーズなどで、リスニングセクションとリーディングセクションの全200問を通して解答してみることをお勧めします。タイマーなどを利用して2時間計測しながら、休憩を入れずに解答しましょう。実際にマークシートを塗って解答練習を行うことも重要です。その際、時間切れにならずに最後の問題まで解答できるよう、リーディングセクションでは時間配分に注意を払いましょう。

Part 1 ～ 4 の問題形式および Directions（指示文）とその訳

本番のテストでは、問題用紙のリスニングセクションの冒頭には、リスニングセクション全体の説明と Part 1 の指示文と例題が、Part 2 ～ 4 の冒頭にはそれぞれのパートの指示文が印刷されており、音声でも流れます。本書の各セクションの学習を始める前にこれらの指示文を読んで音声を聞き、各パートの流れを確認しましょう。

Part 1 写真描写問題

問題数と内容 6 問（Q1 ～ 6）。1 枚の写真を見ながら、4 つの説明文を音声で聞き、写真を最も適切に描写している説明文を選ぶ問題です。4 つの説明文は問題用紙には印刷されていません。

LISTENING TEST

In the Listening test, you will be asked to demonstrate how well you understand spoken English. The entire Listening test will last approximately 45 minutes. There are four parts, and directions are given for each part. You must mark your answers on the separate answer sheet. Do not write your answers in your test book.

PART 1

Directions: For each question in this part, you will hear four statements about a picture in your test book. When you hear the statements, you must select the one statement that best describes what you see in the picture. Then find the number of the question on your answer sheet and mark your answer. The statements will not be printed in your test book and will be spoken only one time.

Look at the example item below.
Now listen to the four statements.
(A) They're moving some furniture.
(B) They're entering a meeting room.
(C) They're sitting at a table.
(D) They're cleaning the carpet.

Statement (C), "They're sitting at a table," is the best description of the picture, so you should select answer (C) and mark it on your answer sheet.

Now Part 1 will begin.

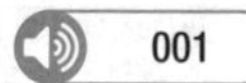

リスニングテスト

リスニングテストでは、話されている英語をどのくらいよく理解しているかが問われます。リスニングテストは全体で約 45 分間です。4 つのパートがあり、各パートにおいて指示が与えられます。答えは、別紙の解答用紙にマークしてください。問題用紙に答えを書き込んではいけません。

パート 1

指示：このパートの各設問では、問題用紙にある写真について、4 つの説明文を聞きます。説明文を聞いて、写真の内容を最も適切に描写しているものを選んでください。そして解答用紙の該当する問題番号にあなたの答えをマークしてください。説明文は問題用紙には印刷されておらず、1 度だけ放送されます。

下の例題を見てください。
では 4 つの説明文を聞きましょう。
(A) 彼らは家具を動かしている。
(B) 彼らは会議室に入ろうとしている。
(C) 彼らはテーブルのところに座っている。
(D) 彼らはカーペットを掃除している。

(C) の文、"They're sitting at a table"「彼らはテーブルのところに座っている」がこの写真を最も適切に描写しているので、(C) を選び、解答用紙にマークします。

ではパート 1 が始まります。

（網掛け部分）は音声のみで、問題用紙には印刷されていません。

Part 2 応答問題

問題数と内容

25 問 (Q7 ～ 31)。1 つの質問または発言と、それに対する 3 つの応答を聞いて、最も適切な応答を選ぶ問題です。質問・発言と 3 つの応答は問題用紙には印刷されていません。

PART 2

Directions: You will hear a question or statement and three responses spoken in English. They will not be printed in your test book and will be spoken only one time. Select the best response to the question or statement and mark the letter (A), (B), or (C) on your answer sheet.

Now let us begin with question number 7.

パート 2

指示：英語による 1 つの質問または発言と、3 つの応答を聞きます。それらは問題用紙には印刷されておらず、1 度だけ放送されます。質問または発言に対して最も適切な応答を選び、解答用紙の (A)、(B)、または (C) にマークしてください。

では問題 7 から始めましょう。

（網掛け部分）は音声のみで、問題用紙には印刷されていません。

Part 3 会話問題

問題数と内容

13 会話、39 問 (Q32 ～ 70)。2 人または 3 人の間で交わされる会話を聞いて、その内容に関する 3 つの設問に答えます。各設問には 4 つの選択肢があり、その中から最も適切な答えを選びます。会話は問題用紙には印刷されていません。設問と 4 つの選択肢のみが印刷されています。設問は音声でも流れます。

PART 3

Directions: You will hear some conversations between two or more people. You will be asked to answer three questions about what the speakers say in each conversation. Select the best response to each question and mark the letter (A), (B), (C), or (D) on your answer sheet. The conversations will not be printed in your test book and will be spoken only one time.

パート 3

指示：2 人あるいはそれ以上の人々の会話を聞きます。各会話の内容に関する 3 つの設問に答えるよう求められます。それぞれの設問について最も適切な答えを選び、解答用紙の (A)、(B)、(C)、または (D) にマークしてください。会話は問題用紙には印刷されておらず、1 度だけ放送されます。

Part 4 説明文問題

問題数と内容

10 トーク、30 問 (Q71 ～ 100)。1 人の話し手によるトークを聞いて、その内容に関する 3 つの設問に答えます。各設問には 4 つの選択肢があり、その中から最も適切な答えを選びます。トークは問題用紙には印刷されていません。設問と 4 つの選択肢のみが印刷されています。設問は音声でも流れます。

PART 4

Directions: You will hear some talks given by a single speaker. You will be asked to answer three questions about what the speaker says in each talk. Select the best response to each question and mark the letter (A), (B), (C), or (D) on your answer sheet. The talks will not be printed in your test book and will be spoken only one time.

パート 4

指示：1 人の話し手によるトークを聞きます。各トークの内容に関する 3 つの設問に答えるよう求められます。それぞれの設問について最も適切な答えを選び、解答用紙の (A)、(B)、(C)、または (D) にマークしてください。トークは問題用紙には印刷されておらず、1 度だけ放送されます。

Section

1

Section 1 の正解数		
1 回目	2 回目	3 回目
月　　日　　　問／ 19 問	月　　日　　　問／ 19 問	月　　日　　　問／ 19 問

Part 1

005

☐ **1.**

Part 2

006

☐ **2.** Mark your answer on your answer sheet.
☐ **3.** Mark your answer on your answer sheet.
☐ **4.** Mark your answer on your answer sheet.
☐ **5.** Mark your answer on your answer sheet.
☐ **6.** Mark your answer on your answer sheet.
☐ **7.** Mark your answer on your answer sheet.

Part 3

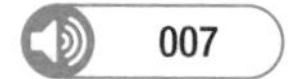

☐ **8.** Where most likely are the speakers?

(A) At a bank
(B) At a law firm
(C) At a hotel
(D) At a shopping center

☐ **9.** What are the speakers preparing for?

(A) A sales presentation
(B) A photo shoot
(C) A training course
(D) A newspaper interview

☐ **10.** What will the speakers most likely do next?

(A) Photocopy some documents
(B) Test some equipment
(C) Make a reservation
(D) Call a client

☐ **11.** What is the conversation mainly about?

(A) Arranging a group tour
(B) Interviewing a job candidate
(C) Confirming business hours
(D) Conducting a training activity

☐ **12.** Why does the man say, “we’re on a strict time schedule”?

(A) To indicate a choice
(B) To ask for assistance
(C) To reassure a manager
(D) To signal the start of a meeting

☐ **13.** What will the man most likely pay extra for?

(A) Security
(B) Transportation
(C) Photographs
(D) Printing

GO ON TO THE NEXT PAGE →

Part 4

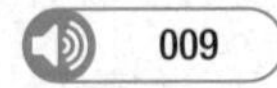

- [ ] **14.** What does the speaker say about the flight?
  - (A) It is a short trip.
  - (B) It is overbooked.
  - (C) It will land soon.
  - (D) It will take a different route.

- [ ] **15.** According to the speaker, what can the flight attendants help with?
  - (A) Completing a form
  - (B) Getting some snacks
  - (C) Finding an assigned seat
  - (D) Checking connecting flights

- [ ] **16.** According to the speaker, what should the listeners do with their belongings?
  - (A) Return them to overhead bins
  - (B) Place them under the seat
  - (C) Secure them in a seat pocket
  - (D) Pick them up at the gate

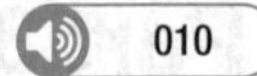

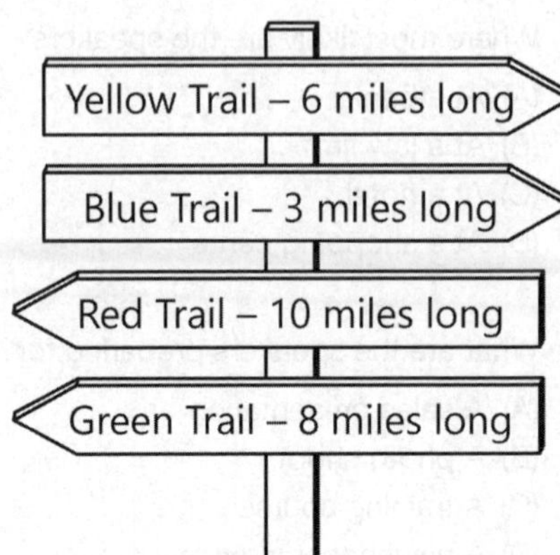

- [ ] **17.** Look at the graphic. Which trail requires some maintenance work?
  - (A) Yellow Trail
  - (B) Blue Trail
  - (C) Red Trail
  - (D) Green Trail

- [ ] **18.** What does the speaker ask the listener to do?
  - (A) Change a task assignment
  - (B) Draw a map
  - (C) Post a notice online
  - (D) Sign some paperwork

- [ ] **19.** Why is the speaker ordering supplies?
  - (A) To create some signs
  - (B) To plant some flower beds
  - (C) To paint some handrails
  - (D) To solve a drainage problem

Section 2

Section 2 の正解数		
1回目	2回目	3回目
月　　日　　　問／19問	月　　日　　　問／19問	月　　日　　　問／19問

Part 1

011

☐ **1.**

Part 2

012

☐ **2.** Mark your answer on your answer sheet.
☐ **3.** Mark your answer on your answer sheet.
☐ **4.** Mark your answer on your answer sheet.
☐ **5.** Mark your answer on your answer sheet.
☐ **6.** Mark your answer on your answer sheet.
☐ **7.** Mark your answer on your answer sheet.

Part 3

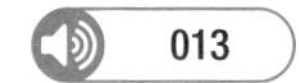

☐ **8.** What activity is scheduled for the morning?

(A) A client meeting
(B) A technology demonstration
(C) A community service fair
(D) A new-employee orientation

☐ **9.** What do the men say they would like to do?

(A) Charge their phones
(B) Register early
(C) Buy some coffee
(D) Take a taxi

☐ **10.** What does the woman say will happen after lunch?

(A) Some badges will be issued.
(B) Log-in passwords will be distributed.
(C) Small-group discussions will be held.
(D) A group photo will be taken.

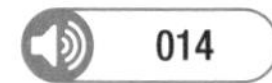

☐ **11.** Why is the woman traveling to Melbourne?

(A) To have a contract signed
(B) To visit some family members
(C) To attend a sports match
(D) To receive an award

☐ **12.** What does the woman imply when she says, "My return flight is on the seventh"?

(A) She has made a change to her travel itinerary.
(B) She needs to reserve ground transportation.
(C) She will not be able to attend an event.
(D) She will not have enough time to go shopping.

☐ **13.** What is the man having trouble deciding on?

(A) A dinner menu
(B) A product name
(C) A location
(D) A gift

GO ON TO THE NEXT PAGE →

Part 4

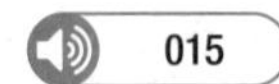

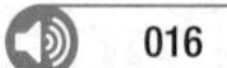

☐ **14.** Where do the listeners work?

(A) At a bank
(B) At a library
(C) At a museum
(D) At a community center

☐ **15.** According to the speaker, what is the purpose of an event?

(A) To promote a new product
(B) To destroy some documents
(C) To recycle old appliances
(D) To raise money for a charity

☐ **16.** What will the listeners receive for volunteering?

(A) A coffee mug
(B) A raffle ticket
(C) A bonus payment
(D) A vacation day

Activity	Guide
Forest walk	Kavi Gupta
Market visit	Vinod Prasad
Rafting adventure	Anil Krishnan
Wildlife sanctuary	Rohan Singh

☐ **17.** What does the speaker say about the listeners' breakfast?

(A) It included local traditional food.
(B) It was prepared by professional chefs.
(C) It was made from healthy ingredients.
(D) It was served buffet style.

☐ **18.** Why was an activity canceled?

(A) Because a park is closing early
(B) Because a guide is unavailable
(C) Because not enough people signed up
(D) Because outdoor conditions are unsuitable

☐ **19.** Look at the graphic. Who is the speaker?

(A) Kavi Gupta
(B) Vinod Prasad
(C) Anil Krishnan
(D) Rohan Singh

Section 3

Section 3 の正解数		
1 回目	2 回目	3 回目
月　日　問／ 19 問	月　日　問／ 19 問	月　日　問／ 19 問

Part 1

017

☐ **1.**

Part 2

018

☐ **2.** Mark your answer on your answer sheet.
☐ **3.** Mark your answer on your answer sheet.
☐ **4.** Mark your answer on your answer sheet.
☐ **5.** Mark your answer on your answer sheet.
☐ **6.** Mark your answer on your answer sheet.
☐ **7.** Mark your answer on your answer sheet.

Part 3

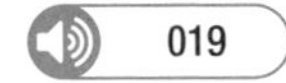

☐ **8.** What are the speakers mainly discussing?

(A) A hiring decision
(B) A training opportunity
(C) A retirement celebration
(D) An account audit

☐ **9.** What does the man highlight about Hans Weber?

(A) He recently won an award.
(B) He has good organizational skills.
(C) He has a lot of experience.
(D) He collaborates well in a team.

☐ **10.** What does the woman say she will do?

(A) Write a report
(B) Check a colleague's availability
(C) Prepare a company announcement
(D) Confirm a venue

☐ **11.** What department do the speakers most likely work in?

(A) Human Resources
(B) Sales
(C) Accounting
(D) Research

☐ **12.** What will be discussed at a meeting?

(A) How much time should be spent on a project
(B) How many interns should be hired
(C) When a product should be launched
(D) Who should complete a performance review

☐ **13.** Why does the woman say, "I can't send the final copy to the director"?

(A) To apologize for her lack of experience
(B) To request assistance from the man
(C) To suggest sending a draft document for review
(D) To clarify an approval process

GO ON TO THE NEXT PAGE →

Part 4

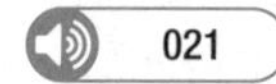

☐ **14.** Why did the speaker choose some software?

(A) It is made by his company.
(B) It is compatible with mobile devices.
(C) It is appropriate for beginners.
(D) It is inexpensive.

☐ **15.** What will the listeners design in today's workshop?

(A) Store signs
(B) Product labels
(C) Event invitations
(D) Magazine covers

☐ **16.** According to the speaker, what can listeners do later?

(A) Sign up for more time
(B) Make a payment
(C) Request a course catalog
(D) Pick up an instruction manual

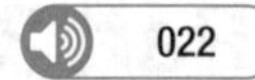

Employee Benefits	
1. Base Weekly Salary	$1,300
2. Sign-on Bonus	$5,000
3. Vacation Days	10 days
4. Personal Days	5 days

☐ **17.** Which industry does the speaker most likely work in?

(A) Energy
(B) Tourism
(C) Transportation
(D) Finance

☐ **18.** What problem is mainly discussed?

(A) Low sales
(B) Outdated equipment
(C) A budget cut
(D) A staff shortage

☐ **19.** Look at the graphic. Which benefit does the speaker recommend changing?

(A) Benefit 1
(B) Benefit 2
(C) Benefit 3
(D) Benefit 4

Section 4

Section 4 の正解数		
1 回目	2 回目	3 回目
月　　日　　　問／ 19 問	月　　日　　　問／ 19 問	月　　日　　　問／ 19 問

Part 1

023

☐ **1.**

Part 2

☐ **2.** Mark your answer on your answer sheet.
☐ **3.** Mark your answer on your answer sheet.
☐ **4.** Mark your answer on your answer sheet.
☐ **5.** Mark your answer on your answer sheet.
☐ **6.** Mark your answer on your answer sheet.
☐ **7.** Mark your answer on your answer sheet.

Part 3

☐ **8.** What type of business does the woman most likely work for?

(A) A shipping company
(B) A boat factory
(C) An automobile mechanic
(D) A fishing tour provider

☐ **9.** What are the men concerned about?

(A) A schedule
(B) An ordering process
(C) Training on safety issues
(D) Transportation to a job site

☐ **10.** What does the woman give to the men?

(A) A pricing pamphlet
(B) A business card
(C) Printed instructions
(D) Some photographs

☐ **11.** Where do the speakers most likely work?

(A) At an accounting firm
(B) At a tourist agency
(C) At an architectural firm
(D) At a software company

☐ **12.** What is the man unsure about?

(A) Meeting a deadline
(B) Making a payment
(C) Revising a contract
(D) Fulfilling a client's request

☐ **13.** Why does the woman say, "I've been having computer problems"?

(A) To justify the purchase of some new office equipment
(B) To offer assistance to a colleague with a technical problem
(C) To explain that some documents have not been reviewed
(D) To criticize an updated company policy

GO ON TO THE NEXT PAGE →

Part 4

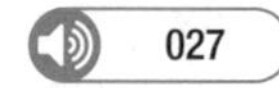

☐ **14.** What is the announcement mainly about?

(A) An early closing
(B) A volunteer opportunity
(C) A music festival
(D) A request for donations

☐ **15.** What does the speaker say about a reception area?

(A) It is next to a lake.
(B) It is under construction.
(C) Large groups can be accommodated.
(D) An invitation is needed for entry.

☐ **16.** What does the speaker say is free today?

(A) Guided tours
(B) A film screening
(C) Parking
(D) Posters

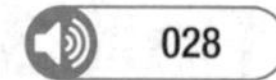

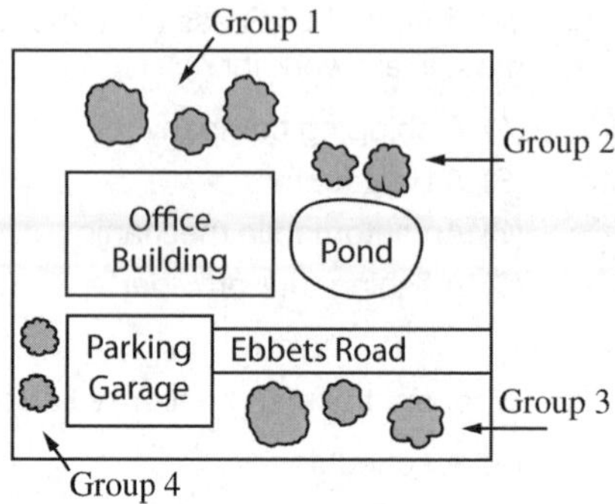

☐ **17.** What is the main purpose of the call?

(A) To explain why a task was not completed
(B) To provide an update on an inspection
(C) To suggest visiting a garden center
(D) To report a staffing change

☐ **18.** Look at the graphic. Which group of trees is the speaker concerned about?

(A) Group 1
(B) Group 2
(C) Group 3
(D) Group 4

☐ **19.** What does the speaker say he will send?

(A) A photograph
(B) A cost estimate
(C) A list of tree varieties
(D) A company brochure

Section
5

Section 5 の正解数		
1 回目	2 回目	3 回目
月　　日　　　問／ 19 問	月　　日　　　問／ 19 問	月　　日　　　問／ 19 問

Part 1

029

☐ **1.**

Part 2

030

☐ **2.** Mark your answer on your answer sheet.
☐ **3.** Mark your answer on your answer sheet.
☐ **4.** Mark your answer on your answer sheet.
☐ **5.** Mark your answer on your answer sheet.
☐ **6.** Mark your answer on your answer sheet.
☐ **7.** Mark your answer on your answer sheet.

Part 3

☐ **8.** What are the speakers discussing?

(A) Scheduling a supply delivery
(B) Hiring temporary workers
(C) Using recycled materials
(D) Moving some equipment

☐ **9.** What is the woman concerned about?

(A) Production delays
(B) Budget limitations
(C) A decline in product quality
(D) A safety regulation

☐ **10.** What does the man say would result from a change?

(A) Energy efficiency would improve.
(B) Employees would be more satisfied.
(C) New products would be created.
(D) Sales would increase.

☐ **11.** What does the factory most likely produce?

(A) Personal electronics
(B) Medical equipment
(C) Kitchen appliances
(D) Engine parts

☐ **12.** What does the woman ask the man about?

(A) The cost of a project
(B) The results of a product test
(C) The location of some new machines
(D) The deadline for an order

☐ **13.** Why does the woman say, "They don't take very long to build"?

(A) To express surprise that a project has not been finished
(B) To suggest using a product that is already in stock
(C) To decline an offer for additional help
(D) To express satisfaction with a production process

GO ON TO THE NEXT PAGE →

Part 4

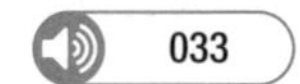

☐ **14.** Who is participating in a city's competition?

(A) High school students
(B) Museum directors
(C) Famous artists
(D) Government officials

☐ **15.** Where will the winning mural be painted?

(A) In a riverfront area
(B) In a shopping district
(C) In a public park
(D) In a school yard

☐ **16.** What are the listeners encouraged to do?

(A) Apply for an open position
(B) Donate some art supplies
(C) Speak with some artists
(D) Help choose a winner

Date: April 25		
Satoshi Ito	3 vanilla cakes	9:00 A.M.
Sakshi Gupta	2 loaves of bread	1:00 P.M.
Maryam Rashad	1 bag of cookies	4:00 P.M.
Felipe Reyes	2 dozen pastries	6:30 P.M.

☐ **17.** What is the purpose of the call?

(A) To inquire about a discount
(B) To complain about service
(C) To schedule a delivery
(D) To explain a delay

☐ **18.** Look at the graphic. What did the speaker order?

(A) Cakes
(B) Bread
(C) Cookies
(D) Pastries

☐ **19.** What did the speaker do last week?

(A) She hosted a party.
(B) She attended a graduation.
(C) She went on a vacation.
(D) She moved into a new apartment.

Section

6

Section 6 の正解数		
1回目	2回目	3回目
月　　日　　問／19問	月　　日　　問／19問	月　　日　　問／19問

Part 1

035

☐ **1.**

Part 2

036

☐ **2.** Mark your answer on your answer sheet.
☐ **3.** Mark your answer on your answer sheet.
☐ **4.** Mark your answer on your answer sheet.
☐ **5.** Mark your answer on your answer sheet.
☐ **6.** Mark your answer on your answer sheet.
☐ **7.** Mark your answer on your answer sheet.

Part 3

☐ **8.** What industry do the speakers most likely work in?

(A) Tourism
(B) Journalism
(C) Music
(D) Film

☐ **9.** What will Martina show the man?

(A) How to load a vehicle
(B) How to clean a vehicle
(C) Where to park a vehicle
(D) Where to pick up a vehicle

☐ **10.** According to Martina, what will there be extra time to do?

(A) Prepare a report
(B) Eat dinner
(C) Conduct an interview
(D) Set up equipment

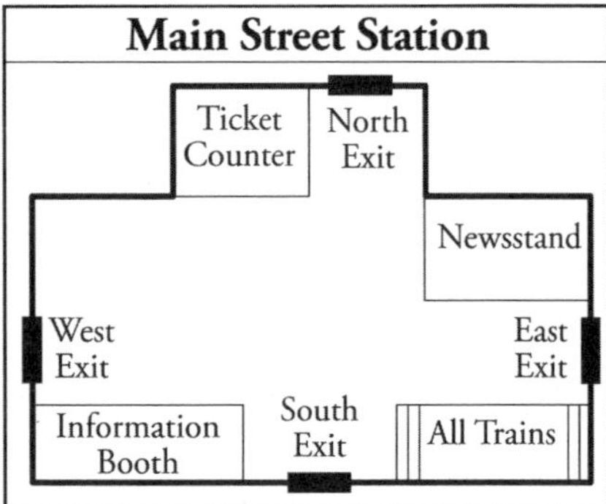

☐ **11.** What will the speakers do at three o'clock?

(A) Participate in a training
(B) Look at an office space
(C) Give a workshop
(D) Inspect a factory

☐ **12.** Look at the graphic. At which exit will the speakers meet?

(A) North
(B) East
(C) South
(D) West

☐ **13.** What does the woman suggest?

(A) Calling a supervisor
(B) Sending a payment
(C) Buying some food
(D) Taking an earlier train

Section 6

GO ON TO THE NEXT PAGE →

Part 4

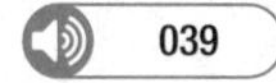

□ **14.** What industry do the listeners work in?

(A) Forestry
(B) Sanitation
(C) Architecture
(D) Manufacturing

□ **15.** What does the speaker imply when he says, "Now there are 24 members"?

(A) A job fair was successful.
(B) A meeting room is too small.
(C) A membership fee will change.
(D) An organization is growing.

□ **16.** What information does the handout contain?

(A) A list of participants
(B) A regional map
(C) The steps of a plan
(D) The results of a study

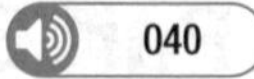

□ **17.** What is the speaker mainly discussing?

(A) A revised production schedule
(B) A new software system
(C) A change in company leadership
(D) An updated vacation policy

□ **18.** According to the speaker, what have the listeners asked about?

(A) The password for a document
(B) The criteria for a job promotion
(C) The reason for a decision
(D) The plan for staff training

□ **19.** What should the listeners do on Friday?

(A) Clean a work space
(B) Complete a checklist
(C) Download an instruction manual
(D) Leave some equipment at the office

Section 7

Section 7 の正解数		
1 回目	2 回目	3 回目
月　日　問／19 問	月　日　問／19 問	月　日　問／19 問

Part 1

041

☐ **1.**

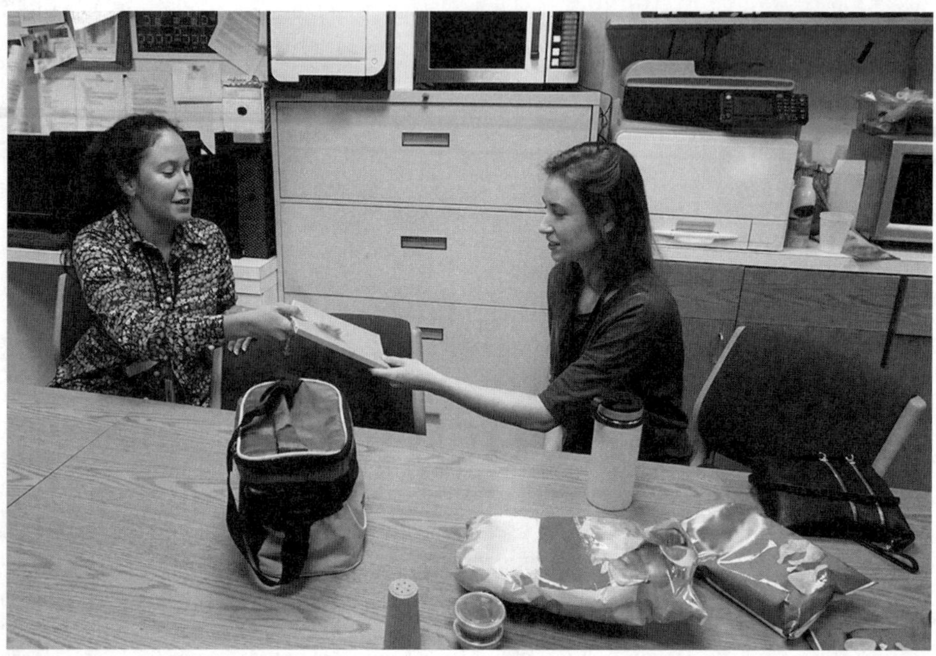

Part 2

042

☐ **2.** Mark your answer on your answer sheet.
☐ **3.** Mark your answer on your answer sheet.
☐ **4.** Mark your answer on your answer sheet.
☐ **5.** Mark your answer on your answer sheet.
☐ **6.** Mark your answer on your answer sheet.
☐ **7.** Mark your answer on your answer sheet.

Part 3

043

☐ **8.** What is the discussion mainly about?

(A) A hiring initiative
(B) A funding request
(C) A process innovation
(D) A product prototype

☐ **9.** What does the woman say she needs?

(A) Some product specifications
(B) Some earnings projections
(C) A manager's approval
(D) An updated timeline

☐ **10.** What does the man plan to do?

(A) Check some references
(B) Compare vendor bids
(C) Arrange a videoconference
(D) Consult a manual

044

Climson Department Store Coupon

10% off $25 or less
15% off $26–$50
20% off $51–$75
25% off $76 and up

Discount off entire purchase

☐ **11.** What does the woman say she did last month?

(A) She went on a vacation.
(B) She organized an event.
(C) She started a new job.
(D) She opened a new business.

☐ **12.** Look at the graphic. What discount does the woman receive?

(A) 10%
(B) 15%
(C) 20%
(D) 25%

☐ **13.** How can the woman win a gift card?

(A) By filling out a survey
(B) By entering a contest
(C) By referring a friend
(D) By signing up for a newsletter

GO ON TO THE NEXT PAGE →

Part 4

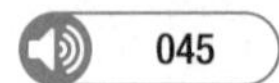

☐ **14.** What will the speaker give to each listener?

(A) A lunch voucher
(B) A reference letter
(C) An identification card
(D) An employment contract

☐ **15.** What does the speaker ask the listeners to check?

(A) The color of a logo
(B) The spelling of a name
(C) The date of a signature
(D) The location of an office

☐ **16.** What will the listeners do after the break?

(A) Try on company uniforms
(B) Log in to e-mail accounts
(C) Pose for a group picture
(D) Go on a tour of the building

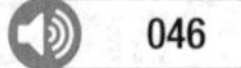

☐ **17.** Where does the speaker work?

(A) At a plastics manufacturing plant
(B) At an electronics company
(C) At a construction firm
(D) At a car repair shop

☐ **18.** Why does the speaker say, "It took three hours to discover the problem"?

(A) To ask for a job transfer
(B) To complain about some colleagues
(C) To request overtime pay
(D) To explain a delayed shipment

☐ **19.** What does the speaker want to discuss at a future meeting?

(A) Some software programs
(B) Some sales reports
(C) A product advertisement
(D) A hiring decision

Section 8

Section 8 の正解数		
1回目	2回目	3回目
月　日　問／19問	月　日　問／19問	月　日　問／19問

Part 1

047

☐ **1.**

Part 2

048

☐ **2.** Mark your answer on your answer sheet.
☐ **3.** Mark your answer on your answer sheet.
☐ **4.** Mark your answer on your answer sheet.
☐ **5.** Mark your answer on your answer sheet.
☐ **6.** Mark your answer on your answer sheet.
☐ **7.** Mark your answer on your answer sheet.

Part 3

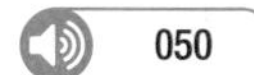

☐ **8.** What event will take place next summer?

(A) A local election
(B) A sports competition
(C) A trade show
(D) A holiday festival

☐ **9.** What does the woman say is the cause of a problem?

(A) A business location
(B) A transportation cost
(C) A weather forecast change
(D) A speaker cancellation

☐ **10.** What suggestion does Thomas make?

(A) Hiring a consultant
(B) Changing an event date
(C) Advertising on television
(D) Offering extra incentives

Clinic Directory

Emiko Sato, Dietitian	Suite 104
Salma Aziz, Fitness Coach	Suite 105
Wu Zhang, Physical Therapist	Suite 106
Anil Ortiz, Health Counselor	Suite 107

☐ **11.** Look at the graphic. Who is the woman's aunt meeting with?

(A) Emiko Sato
(B) Salma Aziz
(C) Wu Zhang
(D) Anil Ortiz

☐ **12.** What does the man ask the woman to do?

(A) Contact a pharmacy
(B) Make an appointment
(C) Sign a visitor's log
(D) Show some identification

☐ **13.** What is the woman most likely going to do next?

(A) Get a parking pass
(B) Wait in a lobby
(C) Make a phone call
(D) Read a pamphlet

Section 8

GO ON TO THE NEXT PAGE →

Part 4

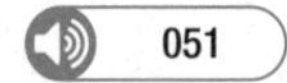

☐ **14.** Which field does the speaker work in?

(A) Marketing
(B) Banking
(C) Real estate
(D) Human resources

☐ **15.** What does the speaker request?

(A) A signature
(B) A photograph
(C) A list of references
(D) A copy of a certificate

☐ **16.** Why does the speaker say, "I work until five today"?

(A) To indicate availability
(B) To accept an invitation
(C) To request assistance
(D) To correct a misunderstanding

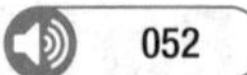

☐ **17.** Why does the speaker mention his father?

(A) To give him credit for a new product idea
(B) To announce a retirement celebration
(C) To question a business decision
(D) To emphasize the company's long history

☐ **18.** What type of product is being described?

(A) Exercise equipment
(B) Cleaning supplies
(C) Healthy snacks
(D) Home improvement tools

☐ **19.** What does the speaker mean when he says, "it's a large order"?

(A) He is asking for assistance with a task.
(B) He is correcting a colleague's misunderstanding.
(C) He is certain that a product line will be successful.
(D) He is concerned about meeting a deadline.

Section 9

Section 9 の正解数		
1 回目	2 回目	3 回目
月　日　問／ 19 問	月　日　問／ 19 問	月　日　問／ 19 問

Part 1

053

☐ **1.**

Part 2

☐ **2.** Mark your answer on your answer sheet.
☐ **3.** Mark your answer on your answer sheet.
☐ **4.** Mark your answer on your answer sheet.
☐ **5.** Mark your answer on your answer sheet.
☐ **6.** Mark your answer on your answer sheet.
☐ **7.** Mark your answer on your answer sheet.

Part 3

☐ **8.** What industry do the speakers most likely work in?

(A) Information technology
(B) Transportation
(C) Finance
(D) Television

☐ **9.** What advantage of a proposal does the woman mention?

(A) Some materials could be sourced locally.
(B) Some trainings could be moved online.
(C) Some useful information could be displayed.
(D) Some project times could be shortened.

☐ **10.** What does the man ask the woman to do?

(A) Print a form
(B) Schedule a meeting
(C) Draft a contract
(D) Issue a payment

PRICE LIST

ITEM	COST
Adjustable wrench	$3.00
Meterstick	$5.00
Rubber mallet	$7.00
Phillips screwdriver	$9.00

☐ **11.** What does the man say he is working on?

(A) Moving some equipment
(B) Painting a room
(C) Assembling some furniture
(D) Repairing an appliance

☐ **12.** Look at the graphic. How much will the man pay for a tool?

(A) $3.00
(B) $5.00
(C) $7.00
(D) $9.00

☐ **13.** What does the woman offer to do?

(A) Confirm a password
(B) Order an item
(C) Report a complaint
(D) Apply a discount

GO ON TO THE NEXT PAGE →

Part 4

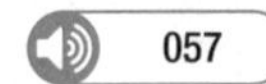

☐ **14.** What does the company sell?

(A) Appliances
(B) Clothing
(C) Software
(D) Books

☐ **15.** What feature of a Web site was recently improved?

(A) How images are displayed
(B) How fast a purchase is made
(C) How product descriptions are written
(D) How easy it is to search for a product

☐ **16.** What does the speaker say she will do at the next meeting?

(A) Present a sales report
(B) Introduce a new employee
(C) Announce promotions
(D) Share survey results

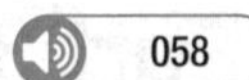

☐ **17.** What are the listeners most likely participating in?

(A) A shareholders meeting
(B) A focus group
(C) A contract negotiation
(D) A management workshop

☐ **18.** According to the speaker, what should the listeners pay attention to?

(A) Some sales figures
(B) Some deadlines
(C) Some photographs
(D) Some packaging

☐ **19.** What does the speaker imply when he says, "the nondisclosure forms are right here"?

(A) He needs to leave early.
(B) He has finished an assignment.
(C) The listeners should complete some documents.
(D) The listeners have already been hired.

Section 10

Section 10 の正解数		
1回目	2回目	3回目
月　日　問／19問	月　日　問／19問	月　日　問／19問

Part 1

059

□ **1.**

Part 2

060

□ **2.** Mark your answer on your answer sheet.
□ **3.** Mark your answer on your answer sheet.
□ **4.** Mark your answer on your answer sheet.
□ **5.** Mark your answer on your answer sheet.
□ **6.** Mark your answer on your answer sheet.
□ **7.** Mark your answer on your answer sheet.

Part 3

061

8. Who most likely are the speakers?
   (A) Doctors
   (B) Electricians
   (C) Architects
   (D) Lab technicians

9. What is scheduled to happen next week?
   (A) A building tour will be given.
   (B) Some walls will be painted.
   (C) New furniture will be delivered.
   (D) A guest lecturer will make a presentation.

10. What does the woman say she will do next?
   (A) Post some signs
   (B) Update a schedule
   (C) Unload materials from a vehicle
   (D) Unlock the door to the laboratory

062

Irina Lachapelle
Employee ID: 1796-021
Department code: 4328

Bar code:

11. Look at the graphic. Which number will the woman enter?
   (A) 1796
   (B) 4328
   (C) 5012
   (D) 3452

12. What happened last week?
   (A) An employee badge was lost.
   (B) A client luncheon was held.
   (C) A safety inspection was conducted.
   (D) A company merger was finalized.

13. Why did the man access the building on Saturday?
   (A) To retrieve his eyeglasses
   (B) To volunteer for an event
   (C) To bring in some artwork
   (D) To prepare for a workshop

GO ON TO THE NEXT PAGE →

Part 4

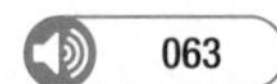

☐ **14.** What field does the speaker most likely work in?

(A) Hospitality
(B) Finance
(C) Real estate
(D) Web-site design

☐ **15.** What does the speaker say she received?

(A) A property brochure
(B) An updated invoice
(C) Some pictures
(D) Some client feedback

☐ **16.** Why does the speaker say, "availability can change quickly"?

(A) To justify a hiring plan
(B) To encourage a prompt reply
(C) To disagree with a recommendation
(D) To apologize for a cancellation

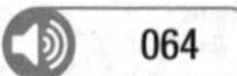

☐ **17.** What does the speaker ask the listeners to do at an entrance?

(A) Pick up some information
(B) Put on protective clothing
(C) Sign a check-in sheet
(D) Leave job applications

☐ **18.** What does the speaker mean when he says, "our production season is from February to April"?

(A) He is not placing any more orders.
(B) He will be unavailable until April.
(C) He is offering jobs for a limited time.
(D) He would like to extend his production season.

☐ **19.** What will the listeners most likely do next?

(A) Taste some samples
(B) Watch a demonstration
(C) Unload a delivery truck
(D) Plant some trees

Section

11

Section 11 の正解数		
1 回目	2 回目	3 回目
月　日　問／ 19 問	月　日　問／ 19 問	月　日　問／ 19 問

Part 1

065

☐ **1.**

Part 2

☐ **2.** Mark your answer on your answer sheet.
☐ **3.** Mark your answer on your answer sheet.
☐ **4.** Mark your answer on your answer sheet.
☐ **5.** Mark your answer on your answer sheet.
☐ **6.** Mark your answer on your answer sheet.
☐ **7.** Mark your answer on your answer sheet.

Part 3

☐ **8.** What type of product is the woman calling about?

(A) Shoes
(B) Hats
(C) Jackets
(D) Skirts

☐ **9.** What does the woman imply when she says, "Radcliffe is two hours away"?

(A) She will need help from a colleague.
(B) She wants to hold an event in Radcliffe.
(C) She does not want to travel to Radcliffe.
(D) She cannot extend a deadline.

☐ **10.** What will the man do next?

(A) Process an order
(B) E-mail a link to a Web site
(C) Correct an error
(D) Speak to a manager

Taylor Print Shop	
Copier Model	
M-20	Basic - Black & White
M-30	Advanced - Black & White
M-50	Basic - Color
M-60	Advanced - Color

☐ **11.** What does the woman need copies of?

(A) A photograph
(B) A concert program
(C) A financial report
(D) A party invitation

☐ **12.** What does the man say about the staff?

(A) They are at a training session.
(B) They are busy with a work task.
(C) They were recently hired.
(D) Their shift is about to end.

☐ **13.** Look at the graphic. Which copier model will the woman probably use?

(A) M-20
(B) M-30
(C) M-50
(D) M-60

GO ON TO THE NEXT PAGE →

Part 4

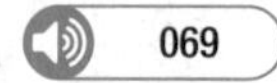

☐ **14.** Who most likely is the listener?

(A) A construction worker
(B) An artist
(C) A hair stylist
(D) A teacher

☐ **15.** According to the speaker, what did the listener ask about?

(A) Whether to bring some materials
(B) Where to meet some colleagues
(C) How to make a payment
(D) When to submit an application

☐ **16.** What does the speaker mean when he says, "our workers are very experienced"?

(A) The workers should receive an increase in salary.
(B) The workers have earned a special certification.
(C) The workers will not damage an item.
(D) The workers are not currently available.

☐ **17.** Who is Elise Weber?

(A) An architect
(B) An author
(C) A filmmaker
(D) A photographer

☐ **18.** What is the Stanton neighborhood known for?

(A) Its scenic views
(B) Its diverse population
(C) Its long history
(D) Its art museum

☐ **19.** Why does the speaker say, "We have a very large crowd today"?

(A) To explain the reason for a problem
(B) To express satisfaction with an advertising campaign
(C) To suggest finding another location
(D) To question a coworker's decision

Section
12

Section 12 の正解数		
1回目	2回目	3回目
月　　日　　　問／19問	月　　日　　　問／19問	月　　日　　　問／19問

Part 1

071

☐ **1.**

Part 2

☐ **2.** Mark your answer on your answer sheet.
☐ **3.** Mark your answer on your answer sheet.
☐ **4.** Mark your answer on your answer sheet.
☐ **5.** Mark your answer on your answer sheet.
☐ **6.** Mark your answer on your answer sheet.
☐ **7.** Mark your answer on your answer sheet.

Part 3

☐ **8.** What is the purpose of the conversation?

(A) To revise a payment process
(B) To discuss an annual report
(C) To plan a charity event
(D) To negotiate a sales contract

☐ **9.** What does the company want to purchase?

(A) Trains
(B) Warehouses
(C) Computers
(D) Boats

☐ **10.** What will the speakers do tomorrow?

(A) Test a product
(B) Train an employee
(C) Meet a government official
(D) Submit a grant request

074

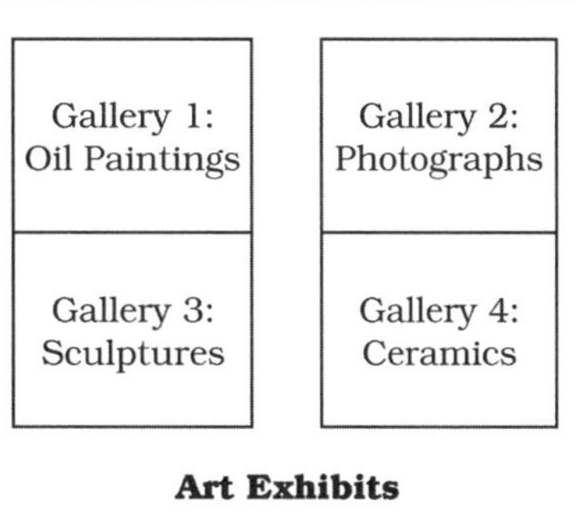

☐ **11.** Why is the man visiting the art museum?

(A) To take a tour
(B) To make a donation
(C) To purchase a gift
(D) To do research for a book

☐ **12.** Look at the graphic. Which gallery does the woman say is currently closed?

(A) Gallery 1
(B) Gallery 2
(C) Gallery 3
(D) Gallery 4

☐ **13.** What does the woman suggest doing?

(A) Taking some private art lessons
(B) Attending a guest lecture
(C) Speaking with a museum director
(D) Viewing an exhibit online

Section 12

GO ON TO THE NEXT PAGE →

Part 4

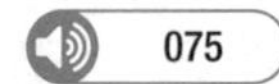

☐ **14.** What event is being celebrated?

(A) A company anniversary
(B) A product launch
(C) A national holiday
(D) A retirement

☐ **15.** According to the speaker, what will the company do after the New Year?

(A) Elect a new board member
(B) Open an office overseas
(C) Merge with another company
(D) Launch an advertising campaign

☐ **16.** What will happen next?

(A) Some prizes will be given out.
(B) Some food will be provided.
(C) A video will be shown.
(D) A band will begin playing.

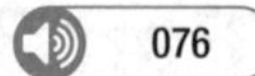

☐ **17.** What type of company does the speaker work for?

(A) An advertising firm
(B) A department store
(C) A law firm
(D) A bank

☐ **18.** Why does the speaker say, "many residential buildings have retail space on the ground floor"?

(A) To explain a decision
(B) To express agreement
(C) To correct an error
(D) To make a suggestion

☐ **19.** According to the speaker, what will happen in two weeks?

(A) A payment will be due.
(B) A committee will meet.
(C) A tour will be given.
(D) A product will be launched.

Section 13

Section 13 の正解数		
1回目	2回目	3回目
月　　日　　　問／ 19 問	月　　日　　　問／ 19 問	月　　日　　　問／ 19 問

Part 1

077

□ **1.**

Part 2

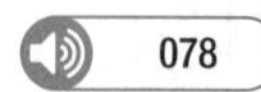

□ **2.** Mark your answer on your answer sheet.
□ **3.** Mark your answer on your answer sheet.
□ **4.** Mark your answer on your answer sheet.
□ **5.** Mark your answer on your answer sheet.
□ **6.** Mark your answer on your answer sheet.
□ **7.** Mark your answer on your answer sheet.

Part 3

079

☐ **8.** What does the woman imply when she says, "I've only had this car for a month"?

(A) She has not used one of her car's features.
(B) She does not want to drive long distances.
(C) She is surprised that a repair is needed.
(D) She is not interested in buying a new car.

☐ **9.** What event are the speakers most likely going to?

(A) A festival
(B) A conference
(C) A training session
(D) A product-release event

☐ **10.** What industry do the speakers most likely work in?

(A) Hospitality
(B) Transportation
(C) News media
(D) Health care

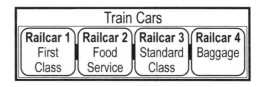

080

Train Cars			
Railcar 1 First Class	**Railcar 2** Food Service	**Railcar 3** Standard Class	**Railcar 4** Baggage

☐ **11.** Look at the graphic. Which railcar are the speakers currently in?

(A) Railcar 1
(B) Railcar 2
(C) Railcar 3
(D) Railcar 4

☐ **12.** What does the man say he needs to do?

(A) Check some tickets
(B) Consult a manager
(C) Make an announcement
(D) Store some luggage

☐ **13.** What does the woman say will happen at the next stop?

(A) A train will change tracks.
(B) Some supplies will be delivered.
(C) A coworker will board the train.
(D) Some maintenance will take place.

GO ON TO THE NEXT PAGE →

Part 4

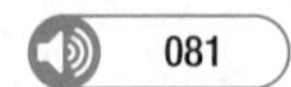

□ **14.** Where does the announcement most likely take place?

(A) At a restaurant
(B) At a supermarket
(C) At a travel agency
(D) At a publishing company

□ **15.** According to the speaker, what will happen on Thursday?

(A) An appliance will be repaired.
(B) A writer will visit.
(C) Some products will be delivered.
(D) Some staff will be trained.

□ **16.** What does the speaker ask the listeners to do?

(A) Pick up a special uniform
(B) Print an order form
(C) Review some instructions
(D) Memorize some names

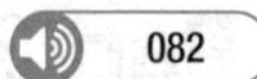

□ **17.** Who most likely is the speaker?

(A) An engineer
(B) An attorney
(C) A banker
(D) An architect

□ **18.** Why does the speaker say, "Many companies are making these changes nowadays"?

(A) To correct a misunderstanding
(B) To express concern about competition
(C) To encourage a purchase
(D) To explain a delay

□ **19.** What will the listeners do next?

(A) Fill out some forms
(B) Watch a video
(C) Put on safety equipment
(D) Tour a building

Section 14

Section 14 の正解数		
1 回目	2 回目	3 回目
月　日　問／ 19 問	月　日　問／ 19 問	月　日　問／ 19 問

Part 1

083

□ **1.**

Part 2

084

□ **2.** Mark your answer on your answer sheet.
□ **3.** Mark your answer on your answer sheet.
□ **4.** Mark your answer on your answer sheet.
□ **5.** Mark your answer on your answer sheet.
□ **6.** Mark your answer on your answer sheet.
□ **7.** Mark your answer on your answer sheet.

Part 3

- [ ] **8.** Who most likely is Hassan?
  - (A) A potential investor
  - (B) A visiting safety inspector
  - (C) A new employee
  - (D) A returning customer

- [ ] **9.** What does the man say is impressive about a boat?
  - (A) It is fast.
  - (B) It is lightweight.
  - (C) It is inexpensive.
  - (D) It is energy efficient.

- [ ] **10.** What does the woman say she will do?
  - (A) Order some supplies
  - (B) Complete a registration form
  - (C) Schedule a payment
  - (D) Provide design information

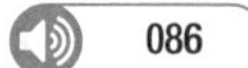

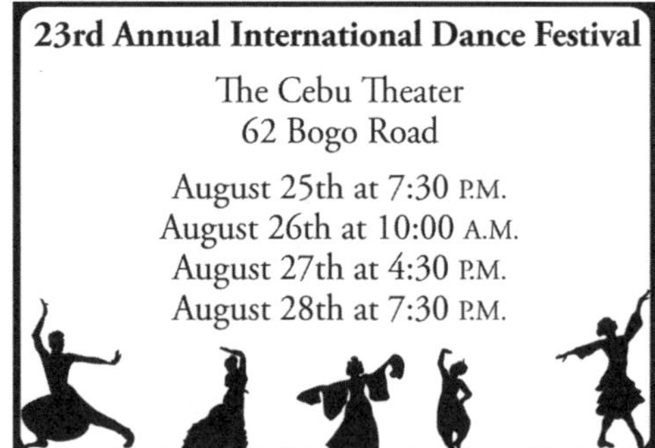

23rd Annual International Dance Festival
The Cebu Theater
62 Bogo Road
August 25th at 7:30 P.M.
August 26th at 10:00 A.M.
August 27th at 4:30 P.M.
August 28th at 7:30 P.M.

- [ ] **11.** What does the woman say about a restaurant?
  - (A) It was noisy.
  - (B) It was expensive.
  - (C) The food was bland.
  - (D) The service was slow.

- [ ] **12.** Look at the graphic. When can the man probably attend a performance?
  - (A) On August 25
  - (B) On August 26
  - (C) On August 27
  - (D) On August 28

- [ ] **13.** What does the man ask the woman to do?
  - (A) Contact a friend
  - (B) Make an appointment
  - (C) Send a photo
  - (D) Buy some tickets

GO ON TO THE NEXT PAGE →

Part 4

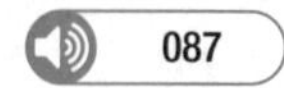

☐ **14.** Why does the speaker say, "Preparations for a show of this size usually take months"?

(A) To request a larger budget
(B) To explain a production delay
(C) To seek out volunteers for a project
(D) To highlight an achievement

☐ **15.** How can the listeners receive a discount?

(A) By making a purchase online
(B) By completing a survey
(C) By posting a review online
(D) By buying tickets for a group

☐ **16.** What will the speaker most likely do next?

(A) Interview a guest
(B) Present an award
(C) Give a weather report
(D) Answer a listener's call

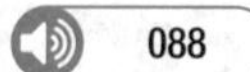

☐ **17.** Who are the listeners?

(A) Factory workers
(B) Maintenance staff
(C) Apartment residents
(D) Office receptionists

☐ **18.** What is the speaker mainly discussing?

(A) How to give feedback
(B) How a facility will be renovated
(C) How packages will be delivered
(D) How to register for a training course

☐ **19.** What advantage of a new system is mentioned?

(A) Wait time will be shortened.
(B) A signature will be unnecessary.
(C) Expenses will be reduced.
(D) A manager will always be available.

Section 15

Section 15 の正解数		
1 回目	2 回目	3 回目
月　日　問／ 19 問	月　日　問／ 19 問	月　日　問／ 19 問

Part 1

089

☐ **1.**

Part 2

☐ **2.** Mark your answer on your answer sheet.
☐ **3.** Mark your answer on your answer sheet.
☐ **4.** Mark your answer on your answer sheet.
☐ **5.** Mark your answer on your answer sheet.
☐ **6.** Mark your answer on your answer sheet.
☐ **7.** Mark your answer on your answer sheet.

Part 3

☐ **8.** What problem does the woman consult the man about?

(A) Some camera batteries will not charge.
(B) A memory card is full.
(C) A carrying case is not big enough.
(D) Some images are not clear.

☐ **9.** What feature does the woman say is important?

(A) The color
(B) The ease of use
(C) The durability
(D) The weight

☐ **10.** What does the man imply when he says, "I'll have to place a special order"?

(A) The woman should choose a different item.
(B) The woman will need to submit a request online.
(C) A product may not be available soon.
(D) A manager's assistance is needed.

Schedule

Time	Room	Client
8:30	109	Wheaton Group
9:30	215	Westover Hotels
10:30	330	Bedichek Alliance
11:30	262	Abidi Medical

☐ **11.** Which industry do the speakers most likely work in?

(A) Banking
(B) Advertising
(C) Technology
(D) Hospitality

☐ **12.** What will the woman do by tomorrow afternoon?

(A) Send a shipment
(B) Confirm a launch date
(C) Finish some revisions
(D) Review some customer feedback

☐ **13.** Look at the graphic. When will a meeting be held?

(A) At 8:30
(B) At 9:30
(C) At 10:30
(D) At 11:30

GO ON TO THE NEXT PAGE →

Part 4

093

☐ **14.** Who is Gerhard Schmidt?

(A) An actor
(B) An architect
(C) An artist
(D) A historian

☐ **15.** What will the listeners do on a tour?

(A) Take a bus trip
(B) Learn about a house
(C) Buy souvenirs
(D) Read historical documents

☐ **16.** Why does the speaker say, "admission to the Schmidt Mansion includes unguided access to the grounds"?

(A) To encourage the listeners to explore the grounds
(B) To inform the listeners of a change in the tour price
(C) To emphasize the need for more tour guides
(D) To promote an audio tour of the grounds

094

☐ **17.** Where does the speaker most likely work?

(A) At a hair salon
(B) At a hotel
(C) At a national park
(D) At an airport

☐ **18.** What is the speaker discussing?

(A) Advertising online
(B) Extending business hours
(C) Hiring some interns
(D) Changing some containers

☐ **19.** What should the listeners encourage customers to do?

(A) Fill out comment cards
(B) Make a reservation
(C) Sign up for a newsletter
(D) Apply for a position

Section 16

Section 16 の正解数		
1回目	2回目	3回目
月　日　問／19問	月　日　問／19問	月　日　問／19問

Part 1

095

□ **1.**

Part 2

096

□ **2.** Mark your answer on your answer sheet.
□ **3.** Mark your answer on your answer sheet.
□ **4.** Mark your answer on your answer sheet.
□ **5.** Mark your answer on your answer sheet.
□ **6.** Mark your answer on your answer sheet.
□ **7.** Mark your answer on your answer sheet.

Part 3

097

- [ ] **8.** Where do the women most likely work?
   (A) At an insurance company
   (B) At an appliance manufacturer
   (C) At a travel agency
   (D) At an accounting firm

- [ ] **9.** Why was the man hired?
   (A) To oversee a recruitment campaign
   (B) To repair some office equipment
   (C) To improve a company's image
   (D) To plan some client-appreciation events

- [ ] **10.** What has Ms. Diaz prepared?
   (A) A promotional brochure
   (B) A manual
   (C) A staff directory
   (D) A presentation

098

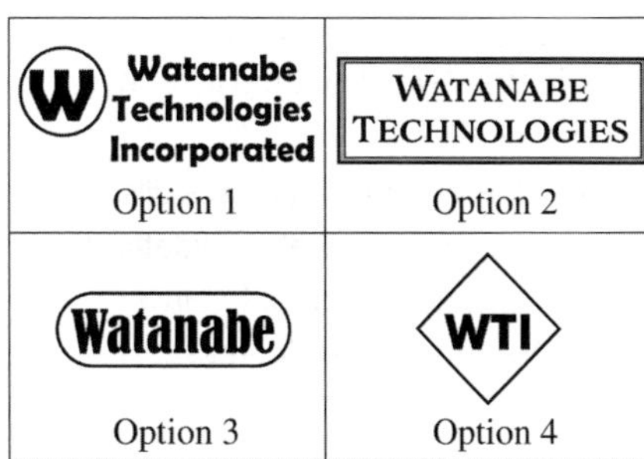

- [ ] **11.** Who most likely is the man?
   (A) A graphic designer
   (B) A company president
   (C) An administrative assistant
   (D) A computer technician

- [ ] **12.** Why did a meeting location change?
   (A) Because a presentation screen is needed
   (B) Because some maintenance work is being done
   (C) Because a larger room was requested
   (D) Because a restaurant does not serve lunch

- [ ] **13.** Look at the graphic. Which logo option does the woman like best?
   (A) Option 1
   (B) Option 2
   (C) Option 3
   (D) Option 4

GO ON TO THE NEXT PAGE →

Part 4

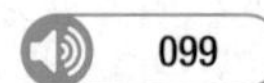

☐ **14.** According to the speaker, what is impressive about the listener's qualifications?

(A) Her foreign language skills
(B) Her professional publications
(C) Her knowledge of tax law
(D) Her advanced degrees

☐ **15.** Who does the speaker want the listener to meet?

(A) A potential client
(B) The director of research
(C) A human resources consultant
(D) The vice president

☐ **16.** What does the speaker say she will arrange for?

(A) A car service
(B) A product delivery
(C) A lunch meeting
(D) A photo session

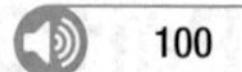

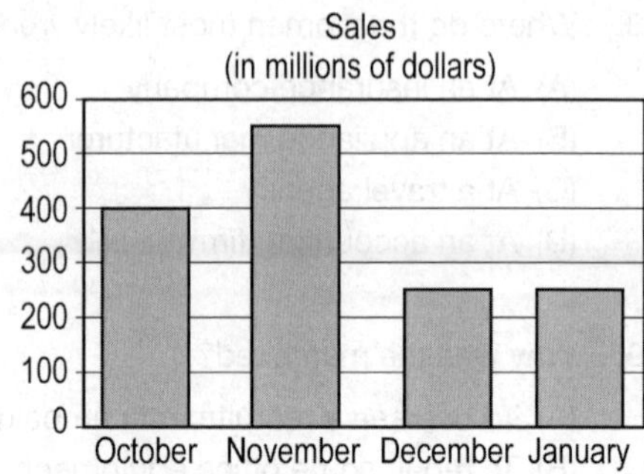

☐ **17.** What does the company sell?

(A) Clothing
(B) Electronics
(C) Beauty products
(D) Sports equipment

☐ **18.** Look at the graphic. During which month did the company hold a promotional event?

(A) October
(B) November
(C) December
(D) January

☐ **19.** What does the speaker suggest?

(A) Offering a discount
(B) Creating a television commercial
(C) Testing some products
(D) Surveying some customers

Section
17

Section 17 の正解数		
1 回目	2 回目	3 回目
月　　日　　　問／ 19 問	月　　日　　　問／ 19 問	月　　日　　　問／ 19 問

Part 1

101

□ **1.**

Part 2

□ **2.** Mark your answer on your answer sheet.
□ **3.** Mark your answer on your answer sheet.
□ **4.** Mark your answer on your answer sheet.
□ **5.** Mark your answer on your answer sheet.
□ **6.** Mark your answer on your answer sheet.
□ **7.** Mark your answer on your answer sheet.

Part 3

103

☐ **8.** Why does the man say, "I've never been there"?

(A) To correct a misunderstanding
(B) To ask for a recommendation
(C) To express surprise
(D) To accept an offer

☐ **9.** What does the man hope that the potential clients will decide to do?

(A) Provide funding for research
(B) Extend their stay in Dallas
(C) Tour a factory
(D) Purchase some machinery

☐ **10.** Why does the woman suggest contacting Vladimir?

(A) He is familiar with the clients.
(B) He is a trained chef.
(C) He is from Dallas.
(D) He has a flexible schedule.

104

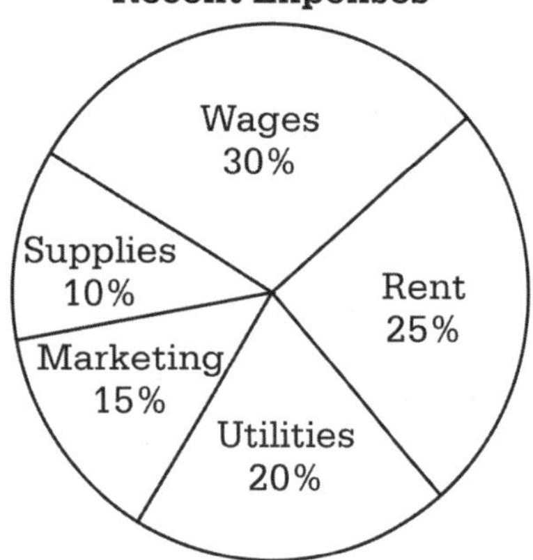

☐ **11.** What type of business do the speakers most likely own?

(A) A grocery store
(B) An electronics shop
(C) A dental clinic
(D) A hair salon

☐ **12.** Look at the graphic. Which percentage of the budget is the woman concerned about?

(A) 30%
(B) 25%
(C) 20%
(D) 15%

☐ **13.** What does the man suggest using some extra money for?

(A) Creating promotional materials
(B) Scheduling a training session
(C) Purchasing new equipment
(D) Hiring additional employees

GO ON TO THE NEXT PAGE →

Part 4

105

106

□ **14.** What type of event are the listeners attending?

(A) An industry conference
(B) A grand opening
(C) A training session
(D) A board meeting

□ **15.** Who is Martina Vogel?

(A) A medical doctor
(B) A news journalist
(C) An airline pilot
(D) A business consultant

□ **16.** According to the speaker, why was Martina Vogel hired?

(A) To design some mobile applications
(B) To address customer complaints
(C) To oversee government regulations
(D) To increase public awareness

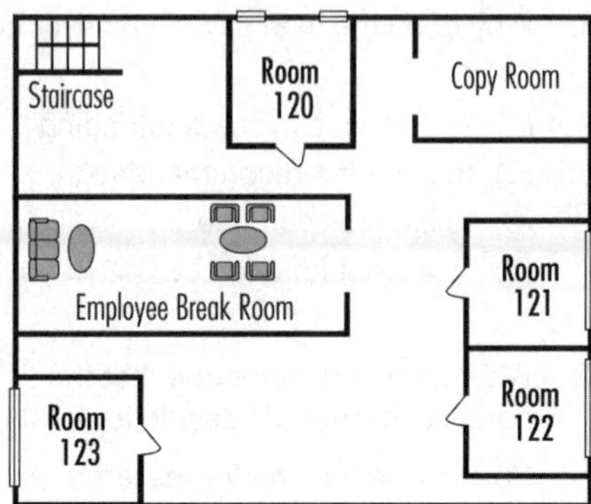

□ **17.** Who are the listeners?

(A) Maintenance staff
(B) Job applicants
(C) Visiting clients
(D) Company interns

□ **18.** Look at the graphic. Which office does the speaker mention?

(A) Room 120
(B) Room 121
(C) Room 122
(D) Room 123

□ **19.** Where will the listeners go after lunch?

(A) To a computer lab
(B) To a security desk
(C) To an auditorium
(D) To an outdoor patio

Section 18

Section 18 の正解数		
1 回目	2 回目	3 回目
月　　日　　　問／ 19 問	月　　日　　　問／ 19 問	月　　日　　　問／ 19 問

Part 1

107

□ **1.**

Part 2

108

□ **2.** Mark your answer on your answer sheet.
□ **3.** Mark your answer on your answer sheet.
□ **4.** Mark your answer on your answer sheet.
□ **5.** Mark your answer on your answer sheet.
□ **6.** Mark your answer on your answer sheet.
□ **7.** Mark your answer on your answer sheet.

Part 3

109

☐ **8.** What are the speakers preparing for?

(A) A board meeting
(B) An annual inspection
(C) A shipment arrival
(D) A sales event

☐ **9.** What will Min Wang do?

(A) Check bar codes
(B) Post signs
(C) Print invoices
(D) Confirm a time

☐ **10.** What does the man need to find?

(A) A sign
(B) A key
(C) Work gloves
(D) A form

110

E-mail Inbox

Davis, Helen Sales update	August 24
Davis, Helen Budget review	August 17
Davis, Helen Project planning	August 10
Davis, Helen Staffing decisions	August 3

☐ **11.** Why has the man not seen his e-mails this morning?

(A) He has been on vacation.
(B) He arrived at the office late.
(C) His computer is being repaired.
(D) His Internet service is not working.

☐ **12.** Look at the graphic. Which meeting will be canceled?

(A) The sales update meeting
(B) The budget review meeting
(C) The project planning meeting
(D) The staffing decisions meeting

☐ **13.** What does the man say about his coworkers?

(A) They have been helpful.
(B) They are very busy.
(C) They are looking forward to a picnic.
(D) They will attend a training session.

GO ON TO THE NEXT PAGE →

Part 4

111

☐ **14.** What event does the speaker mention?

(A) An award ceremony
(B) A theater performance
(C) A press conference
(D) A trade show

☐ **15.** What does the speaker say she likes about the center?

(A) The technical support
(B) The shuttle service
(C) The summer discounts
(D) The spacious rooms

☐ **16.** What does the speaker request?

(A) A cost estimate
(B) A tour of a building
(C) An informational pamphlet
(D) A catering recommendation

112

Calendar

JANUARY	FEBRUARY
Theme: Start-ups	Theme: Leadership
MARCH	**APRIL**
Theme: Social Media	Theme: Small Business

☐ **17.** Where does the speaker most likely work?

(A) At a business school
(B) At a community center
(C) At an employment agency
(D) At a magazine publishing company

☐ **18.** Look at the graphic. Which month's theme will change?

(A) January
(B) February
(C) March
(D) April

☐ **19.** According to the speaker, what is the next step?

(A) Contacting advertisers
(B) Interviewing business experts
(C) Assigning work responsibilities
(D) Posting information on a Web site

Section 19

Section 19 の正解数		
1回目	2回目	3回目
月　　日　　　問／19問	月　　日　　　問／19問	月　　日　　　問／19問

Part 1

113

□ **1.**

Part 2

114

□ **2.** Mark your answer on your answer sheet.
□ **3.** Mark your answer on your answer sheet.
□ **4.** Mark your answer on your answer sheet.
□ **5.** Mark your answer on your answer sheet.
□ **6.** Mark your answer on your answer sheet.
□ **7.** Mark your answer on your answer sheet.

Part 3

115

☐ **8.** Where do the speakers most likely work?

(A) At a clothing company
(B) At a software company
(C) At a shipping company
(D) At a publishing company

☐ **9.** What problem does the woman mention?

(A) Some employees are quitting.
(B) Some customers are complaining.
(C) Some warehouses are closing.
(D) Some computer servers are down.

☐ **10.** What does Carlos suggest researching?

(A) The availability of loans
(B) The popularity of a design
(C) The cost of a change
(D) The advantages of a location

116

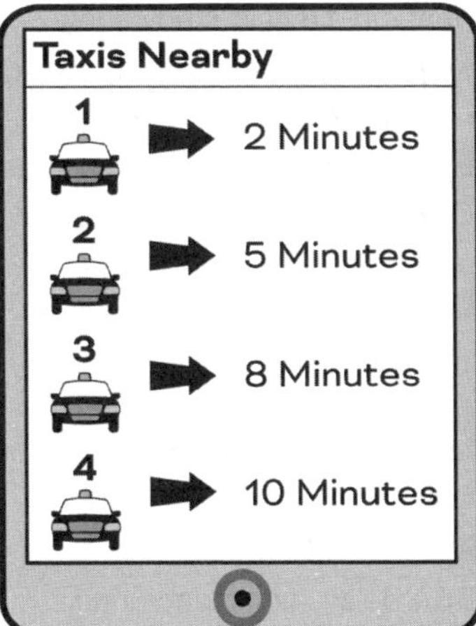

☐ **11.** What event did the speakers attend?

(A) A job fair
(B) A publishing trade show
(C) A retirement party
(D) A museum opening

☐ **12.** What does the woman say she wants to do?

(A) Read a news article
(B) Visit a bookstore
(C) Purchase some food
(D) Reserve a flight

☐ **13.** Look at the graphic. Which taxi will the speakers request?

(A) Taxi 1
(B) Taxi 2
(C) Taxi 3
(D) Taxi 4

GO ON TO THE NEXT PAGE →

Part 4

117

☐ **14.** What did a recent study show?

(A) More business is being conducted online.
(B) Traffic congestion has increased.
(C) Employees prefer a flexible work schedule.
(D) Office equipment should be upgraded regularly.

☐ **15.** According to the speaker, what problem is an industry experiencing?

(A) A loss of revenue
(B) A delay in manufacturing
(C) A decrease in product quality
(D) A lack of qualified employees

☐ **16.** According to the speaker, what change is being considered?

(A) Moving to a new location
(B) Updating a company Web site
(C) Using more energy-efficient models
(D) Allowing employees to work from home

118

Contact	Team
Wei Zhou	Blue
Aisha Osman	Green
Rita Lopez	Yellow
Kavi Krishnan	Orange

☐ **17.** What department does the speaker work in?

(A) Human Resources
(B) Information Technology
(C) Payroll Services
(D) Facility Management

☐ **18.** What is the speaker discussing?

(A) A health program
(B) An orientation schedule
(C) A company-wide meeting
(D) A sales contest

☐ **19.** Look at the graphic. Who does the speaker say some employees should contact?

(A) Wei Zhou
(B) Aisha Osman
(C) Rita Lopez
(D) Kavi Krishnan

Section 20

Section 20 の正解数

1回目	2回目	3回目
月　　日　　　問／19問	月　　日　　　問／19問	月　　日　　　問／19問

Part 1

119

☐ **1.**

Part 2

120

☐ **2.** Mark your answer on your answer sheet.
☐ **3.** Mark your answer on your answer sheet.
☐ **4.** Mark your answer on your answer sheet.
☐ **5.** Mark your answer on your answer sheet.
☐ **6.** Mark your answer on your answer sheet.
☐ **7.** Mark your answer on your answer sheet.

Part 3

121

☐ **8.** What are the speakers discussing?

(A) A job fair
(B) A music concert
(C) A seasonal sale
(D) A sporting event

☐ **9.** What does the woman mean when she says, "people have been in line for hours"?

(A) An event is very popular.
(B) Additional workers are needed.
(C) Refreshments are no longer available.
(D) It is taking a long time to receive information.

☐ **10.** What will the man do next?

(A) Post some signs
(B) Distribute some flyers
(C) Conduct an interview
(D) Take some photographs

122

Level 1	A New World
Level 2	Exploring Atlantis
Level 3	Big Boss Challenge
Level 4	Desert Race
Level 5	Final Showdown

☐ **11.** What was the woman surprised at?

(A) The amount of user feedback
(B) The increase in product sales
(C) A new approach to graphic design
(D) A problem with a merchandising contract

☐ **12.** Look at the graphic. Which level does the man say he will work on?

(A) Level 2
(B) Level 3
(C) Level 4
(D) Level 5

☐ **13.** What will be discussed with the marketing team later?

(A) Advertising posters
(B) Team assignments
(C) A deadline
(D) A product name

GO ON TO THE NEXT PAGE →

Part 4

123

☐ **14.** Who is the speaker?

(A) A news reporter
(B) An environmental activist
(C) A train conductor
(D) A transportation engineer

☐ **15.** Why does the speaker say, "several people were on the team"?

(A) To deny responsibility for an error
(B) To reject a request for a new deadline
(C) To recognize others' contributions
(D) To suggest a new strategy for the future

☐ **16.** What does the speaker say will happen during phase two of a project?

(A) A new payment system will be installed.
(B) Some stations will be renovated.
(C) Some extra workers will be hired.
(D) Additional transit routes will be established.

124

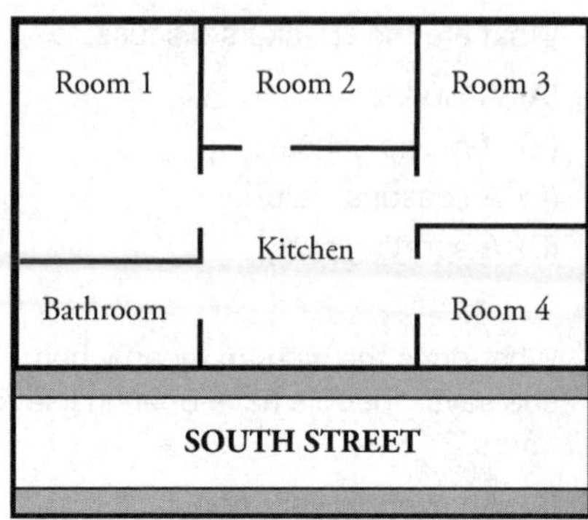

☐ **17.** Why is the speaker unhappy with her current apartment?

(A) It is small.
(B) It is expensive.
(C) It is far from downtown.
(D) It needs some repairs.

☐ **18.** Look at the graphic. Which room does the speaker offer to take?

(A) Room 1
(B) Room 2
(C) Room 3
(D) Room 4

☐ **19.** According to the speaker, what needs to be submitted by Friday?

(A) A contact information form
(B) A deposit
(C) Letters of reference
(D) Proof of employment

公式 TOEIC® Listening & Reading トレーニング 2
リスニング編

2023 年 12 月 6 日　第 1 版第 1 刷発行

著者　ETS

編集協力　株式会社 エディット
株式会社 群企画
株式会社 WIT HOUSE

表紙デザイン　山崎 聡

発行元　一般財団法人 国際ビジネスコミュニケーション協会
〒 100-0014
東京都千代田区永田町 2-14-2
山王グランドビル
電話　(03) 5521-5935

印刷・製本　日経印刷株式会社

Printed in Japan
ISBN 978-4-906033-72-0

公式TOEIC® Listening & Reading トレーニング 2

リスニング編

別冊

正解／スクリプト／訳

公式TOEIC® Listening & Reading トレーニング

リスニング編

別冊

正解／スクリプト／訳

一般財団法人 国際ビジネスコミュニケーション協会

ETS TOEIC® OFFICIAL TEST PREPARATION AND LEARNING

目　次

別冊　正解／スクリプト／訳

Section 1 ······ 3
Section 2 ······ 9
Section 3 ······ 15
Section 4 ······ 21
Section 5 ······ 27
Section 6 ······ 33
Section 7 ······ 39
Section 8 ······ 45
Section 9 ······ 51
Section 10 ······ 57
Section 11 ······ 63
Section 12 ······ 69
Section 13 ······ 75
Section 14 ······ 81
Section 15 ······ 87
Section 16 ······ 93
Section 17 ······ 99
Section 18 ······ 105
Section 19 ······ 111
Section 20 ······ 117

Section 1 正解／スクリプト／訳

正解一覧

Part 1	1 (B)					
Part 2	2 (A)	3 (C)	4 (C)	5 (B)	6 (B)	7 (B)
Part 3	8 (C)	9 (A)	10 (B)	11 (A)	12 (A)	13 (B)
Part 4	14 (C)	15 (A)	16 (B)	17 (C)	18 (A)	19 (C)

Part 1

1. Look at the picture marked number 1 in your test book.
問題用紙の 1 の写真を見てください。

M
(A) The man is signing some papers.
男性は書類にサインしている。
(B) A cash register drawer is open.
レジの引き出しが開いている。
(C) The man is giving out business cards.
男性は名刺を配っている。
(D) A bottle of soda is on a counter.
炭酸飲料のボトルがカウンターの上にある。

Part 2

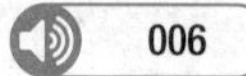

2. W Where should I put these boxes? この箱をどこに置けばいいですか。

M (A) In the back room, please. 奥の部屋にお願いします。
(B) Probably the new office supplies. おそらく新しい事務用品でしょう。
(C) They should, too. 彼らもそうすべきです。

3. M Did you take the train to get here? 電車でこちらにいらしたのですか。

W (A) That's a good price. いい値段ですね。
(B) OK, I'll meet you there. 分かりました、そこで会いましょう。
(C) No, I drove. いいえ、車を運転して来ました。

4. M Who's organizing the author's book signing? 誰が著者のサイン会を取り仕切っていますか。

M (A) On the bookshelf? 本棚の上では?
(B) No, by five o'clock tomorrow. いいえ、明日の5時までにです。
(C) I'm managing the event. 私がその会を運営しています。

5. W Should I print the receipt or e-mail it to you? 領収書は印刷した方がよろしいですか、それともEメールでお送りしましょうか。

W (A) She lost the ticket. 彼女はチケットをなくしました。
(B) I prefer e-mail. Eメールがいいです。
(C) See you next week. 来週お会いしましょう。

6. M Why do we have training materials for only twelve people? なぜ研修資料が12人分しかないのですか。

W (A) We should leave on the thirteenth. 私たちは13日に出発するべきです。
(B) Here's a list of the attendees. こちらが出席者リストです。
(C) I'd prefer to take the bus. 私はバスで行く方がいいです。

7. W What can we do to promote worker productivity? 当社は従業員の生産性を高めるために何ができますか。

M (A) I think that'll work. それでうまくいくと思います。
(B) I can do some research. 私が少し調査してみます。
(C) Yes, he deserves the promotion. はい、彼は昇進して当然です。

Part 3

007

Questions 8 through 10 refer to the following conversation.

問題 8-10 は次の会話に関するものです。

W Hi, William! I'm glad you made it here safely. Did you already check into your room?

お疲れさま、William! あなたが無事に到着してよかったです。もう部屋にチェックインしましたか。

M Not yet. My room isn't ready. That's why I'm sitting here in the lobby practicing our sales pitch for tomorrow's meeting.

まだです。私の部屋はまだ準備できていないのです。だから、こうしてロビーに座って、明日の会議用のセールストークの練習をしているのです。

W I need to review it, too. This presentation's so important. Securing a deal with Istanbul Footwear would be great for our company.

私もそれを見直す必要がありますね。このプレゼンテーションはとても重要です。Istanbul 靴社との契約が決まったら、当社にとって素晴らしいことです。

M Right — I hope we can convince them to sell our shoe brand in their stores.

その通りです——彼らの店舗で当社の靴ブランドを販売してもらえるよう説得できるといいですね。

W Hmm, I wonder if we could get into the meeting room to test the projector and sound system.

ふーむ、私たち、会議室に入ってプロジェクターと音響システムをテストできないでしょうか。

M I already asked someone at the front desk. They said we could test the equipment anytime.

もうフロントの人に聞きましたよ。いつでも機材のテストをしていいと言っていました。

W OK — let's do it now, then.

了解です——では、今すぐやりましょう。

8. 話し手たちはどこにいると思われますか。

(A) 銀行
(B) 法律事務所
(C) ホテル
(D) ショッピングセンター

9. 話し手たちは何の用意をしていますか。

(A) 営業のプレゼンテーション
(B) 写真撮影
(C) 研修講座
(D) 新聞取材

10. 話し手たちは次に何をすると思われますか。

(A) 書類をコピーする
(B) 機材をテストする
(C) 予約を入れる
(D) 顧客に電話する

008

Questions 11 through 13 refer to the following conversation.

問題 11-13 は次の会話に関するものです。

W Sunnyside Tours. How can I help you?

Sunnyside旅行社です。どのようなご用件でしょうか。

M Hi, I'll be in town with some staff for a convention next week, and I'd like to plan a group activity.

こんにちは、来週協議会のためにスタッフ数名で町を訪れます。それで、グループ・アクティビティーを計画したいと思っているんです。

W Sure. Our most popular tour is an all-day trip out to the seaside. But we also have a highly rated historic city tour that lasts just two hours.

かしこまりました。当社の一番人気のツアーは、海辺に出掛ける 1 日ツアーです。しかし、2 時間しかかからない大好評の旧市街ツアーもございます。

M Hmm. They both sound great, but we're on a strict time schedule.

ふーむ。どちらもすごく良さそうですが、スケジュールが厳しいもので。

W I see. Well, I'm sure everyone will enjoy the city tour.

そうですか。でしたら、きっと皆さん市街ツアーをお楽しみいただけると思いますよ。

M Can you provide transportation from our hotel?

宿泊先のホテルから送迎はしてもらえますか。

W Yes, we can provide shuttle service for an extra fee.

はい、追加料金にてシャトルサービスをご提供することができます。

11. この会話は主に何に関するものですか。

(A) グループツアーの手配
(B) 就職希望者の面接
(C) 営業時間の確認
(D) 研修活動の実施

12. 男性はなぜ "we're on a strict time schedule" と言っていますか。

(A) 選択を示すため
(B) 援助を求めるため
(C) 上司を安心させるため
(D) 会議開始を合図するため

13. 男性は何に対して追加料金を支払うと思われますか。

(A) 警備
(B) 移動手段
(C) 写真
(D) 印刷

Part 4

Questions 14 through 16 refer to the following announcement.

問題 14-16 は次のお知らせに関するものです。

M Good afternoon. This is your captain speaking. We'll be landing in Chicago in about fifteen minutes, so please keep your seat belt fastened for the remainder of the flight. If you still need assistance with filling out your customs form, press the green button on your armrest and a flight attendant will come help you. At this time, please secure all loose belongings under the seat in front of you. Thank you for your compliance.

こんにちは。こちら、当便の機長です。あと約 15 分でシカゴに着陸いたしますので、残りの飛行時間中はシートベルトを締めたままでお過ごしください。税関申告書のご記入でまだ手助けが必要な方は、肘掛けの緑色のボタンを押していただくと、客室乗務員がお手伝いに参ります。いま一度、全ての固定されていないお手荷物は前の座席の下にしっかり収納してください。ご協力ありがとうございます。

14. 話し手はこのフライトについて何と言っていますか。

(A) 短時間の飛行である。
(B) 重複して予約されている。
(C) 間もなく着陸する。
(D) 別のルートを取る。

15. 話し手によると、客室乗務員は何を手伝うことができますか。

(A) 用紙に記入すること
(B) 軽食をもらうこと
(C) 指定の席を探すこと
(D) 乗り継ぎ便を確認すること

16. 話し手によると、聞き手たちは手荷物をどうするべきですか。

(A) 頭上の荷物入れに戻す
(B) 座席の下に置く
(C) 座席ポケットに固定する
(D) 搭乗ゲートで受け取る

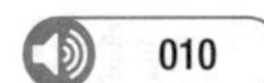

Questions 17 through 19 refer to the following telephone message and signs.

M Hi, it's Dmitry. Since there were strong winds in the area on Sunday night, I walked all the hiking trails over the last two days to look for damage. The shorter trails are in good shape, but the longest trail has several branches blocking the path. I'm going to need some extra help before it can be safely reopened to hikers. Could you schedule the maintenance team to work on that for a few hours today instead of planting the flower beds by the visitors' center? I also noticed that the handrails on a few bridges need to be repainted. I'm putting in an order for some paint so that can be done.

問題 17-19 は次の電話のメッセージと標識に関するものです。

もしもし、Dmitry です。日曜日の夜、この一帯に強風が吹いたので、私はこの2日間で全てのハイキングコースを歩いて被害がないか見てみました。短い方の3つのコースは良い状態ですが、一番長いコースは何本かの枝が道をふさいでいます。ハイカーたちに対してコースを安全に再開できるようにするまでにはもう少し助けが必要です。保守チームに今日、案内所近くの花壇の植栽ではなく、数時間その作業をしてもらえるように予定を組んでいただけますか。私は幾つかの橋の手すりを塗り直す必要があることにも気付きました。その作業ができるようにペンキを注文しておきます。

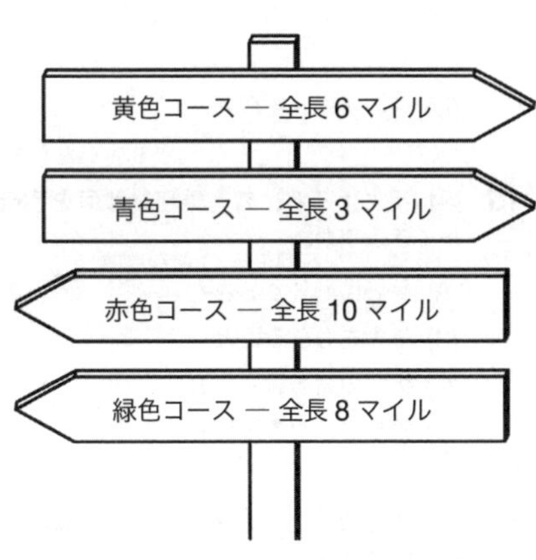

17. 図を見てください。どのコースで保守作業が必要ですか。

(A) 黄色コース
(B) 青色コース
(C) 赤色コース
(D) 緑色コース

18. 話し手は聞き手に何をするよう頼んでいますか。

(A) 作業の割り当てを変更する
(B) 地図を描く
(C) インターネット上にお知らせを出す
(D) 書類に署名する

19. なぜ話し手は備品を注文するのですか。

(A) 標識を作るため
(B) 花壇に植栽するため
(C) 手すりを塗装するため
(D) 排水の問題を解決するため

Section 2 正解／スクリプト／訳

正解一覧

Part 1	1 (D)					
Part 2	2 (A)	3 (C)	4 (A)	5 (C)	6 (B)	7 (B)
Part 3	8 (D)	9 (C)	10 (A)	11 (A)	12 (C)	13 (D)
Part 4	14 (A)	15 (B)	16 (D)	17 (A)	18 (D)	19 (C)

Part 1

1. Look at the picture marked number 1 in your test book.
問題用紙の 1 の写真を見てください。

 W
(A) He's picking up a ladder. 彼ははしごを取り出している。
(B) He's filling a bucket with water. 彼はバケツを水で満たしている。
(C) He's cleaning a display case. 彼は展示ケースを掃除している。
(D) He's mopping the floor. 彼は床にモップをかけている。

Part 2

2. M How much does this digital camera cost? このデジタルカメラは幾らしますか。

W (A) It's 300 euros. 300 ユーロです。
(B) The wide-angle lens. 広角レンズです。
(C) The other ones are. その他のものです。

3. M Are you flying in today or tomorrow? 飛行機でのご到着は今日ですか、明日ですか。

W (A) At terminal three. 第 3 ターミナルで。
(B) Sure, I'll send you the files. いいですよ、ファイルをお送りします。
(C) Today at six o'clock. 今日の 6 時です。

4. W Why were you late this morning? 今朝はなぜ遅刻したのですか。

W (A) Because I missed the bus. バスに乗り遅れたからです。
(B) Thanks, it was great. ありがとう、素晴らしかったです。
(C) At eleven o'clock. 11 時に。

5. W Would you like something to drink? お飲み物はいかがですか。

W (A) We really enjoyed that movie. あの映画は本当に面白かったです。
(B) Pink is my favorite color. ピンクが私のお気に入りの色です。
(C) Sure, I'll have some tea. はい、紅茶をください。

6. W Why are the assembly machines running so slowly? なぜ組立機械の動作がこんなに遅いのですか。

M (A) That's a good suggestion. それはいい提案です。
(B) They'll be inspected tomorrow. 明日、それらの点検が行われることになっています。
(C) On the ground floor. 1 階にあります。

7. M Weren't the new business cards delivered yet? 新しい名刺はまだ届いていなかったのですか。

W (A) The delivery driver. 配達の運転手です。
(B) I'd better call the print shop. 印刷所に電話したほうがいいですね。
(C) The current layout. 現状のレイアウトです。

Part 3

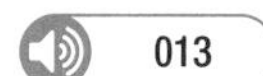

Questions 8 through 10 refer to the following conversation with three speakers.

問題 8-10 は 3 人の話し手による次の会話に関するものです。

W Hello, Jerome and Antonio. I'm Hiroko from Human Resources. In a few minutes, I'll be walking you over to this morning's orientation for new hires.

こんにちは、Jerome と Antonio。人事部の Hiroko です。もう少ししたら、あなた方を午前の新入社員説明会にご案内します。

M1 Great, thanks. I'm wondering. Is there enough time for us to pick up a quick cup of coffee from the cafeteria on the way?

分かりました、ありがとうございます。あのう、途中、カフェテリアでさっとコーヒーを 1 杯買うくらいの時間はあるでしょうか。

M2 Yes, I could really use some coffee, too!

ええ、私もコーヒーが飲めればすごくありがたいです！

W Sure, no problem. The orientation will last about two hours, and then after lunch, you'll be issued your identification badges at the security office.

もちろん、問題ありません。説明会は約 2 時間かかる予定です、それから昼食の後、皆さんは保安課で社員証の発行を受けることになっています。

8. どんな活動が午前中に予定されていますか。

(A) 顧客との打ち合わせ
(B) テクノロジー機器の実演
(C) 社会奉仕バザー
(D) 新入社員説明会

9. 男性たちは何をしたいと言っていますか。

(A) 携帯電話を充電する
(B) 早く登録手続きをする
(C) コーヒーを買う
(D) タクシーに乗る

10. 女性は昼食の後に何があると言っていますか。

(A) 社員証が発行される。
(B) ログインパスワードが配布される。
(C) 小グループの討議が行われる。
(D) 集合写真が撮られる。

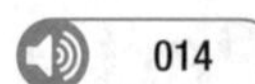

Questions 11 through 13 refer to the following conversation.

問題 11-13 は次の会話に関するものです。

M Jennifer, it's impressive that you're getting Claudine Schmidt to represent our new sports drink. She's one of the biggest soccer stars in the country!

Jennifer、新しいスポーツ飲料の広告モデルを Claudine Schmidt に引き受けてもらうなんてすごいですね。彼女はこの国で最も有名なサッカーのスター選手の一人ですよ！

W Thanks! I'm flying to Melbourne next week with the contract for her to sign. It's been a lot of work, but exciting. By the way… the dinner party for George's retirement is coming up, right?

ありがとう！来週メルボルンに飛んで、彼女に契約書にサインしてもらいます。いろいろと大変だったけど、わくわくしますね。ところで…George の退職ディナーパーティーがもうすぐですよね？

M Yes, on Friday, the third. Can you join us?

はい、3 日の金曜日です。参加できますか。

W My return flight is on the seventh. Is there anything I can help you with before I leave?

帰りのフライトが 7 日なんです。出発する前に私が何か手伝えることはありますか。

M Actually — there's something I need help with now. Do you have any advice on a present for George? I really can't decide on one.

実は――今助けてほしいことがあります。George へのプレゼントに関して何かアドバイスはありますか。私にはどうしても決められないのです。

11. なぜ女性はメルボルンへ行くのですか。

(A) 契約書にサインしてもらうため
(B) 家族を訪ねるため
(C) スポーツの試合を観戦するため
(D) 賞を受け取るため

12. 女性は "My return flight is on the seventh" という発言で、何を示唆していますか。

(A) 彼女は出張の日程を変更した。
(B) 彼女は地上交通機関を予約する必要がある。
(C) 彼女はイベントに出席できない。
(D) 彼女は買い物に行く十分な時間はない。

13. 男性は何を決めるのに困っていますか。

(A) ディナーのメニュー
(B) 製品名
(C) 場所
(D) 贈り物

Part 4

015

Questions 14 through 16 refer to the following excerpt from a meeting.

問題 14-16 は次の会議の一部に関するものです。

W Before we end our staff meeting, I want to remind everyone that our bank branch is hosting a document-shredding event. If you haven't participated before, the bank is renting a commercial paper shredder. Customers and community members can bring in confidential documents they want destroyed, like old bank records, receipts, or pay stubs. The event's next Saturday, and we're still short a few helpers. Remember, everyone who volunteers will earn one extra vacation day. The sign-up sheet's on my desk.

スタッフ会議を終える前に、当銀行支店が文書破棄イベントを開催する予定であることを皆さんに再度お伝えしておきたいと思います。これまでに参加したことがなければご説明すると、当行が業務用シュレッダーを賃借します。お客さまや地域の方々には古い口座取引記録、領収書、給与明細など、破棄したい秘密文書をご持参いただけます。イベントは次の土曜日ですが、まだ数名助け手が足りておりません。忘れないでくださいね、手伝いを申し出てくれた方全員が追加の休暇を 1 日獲得しますよ。申込用紙は私の机の上にあります。

14. 聞き手たちはどこで働いていますか。

(A) 銀行
(B) 図書館
(C) 美術館
(D) 地域の公民館

15. 話し手によると、イベントの目的は何ですか。

(A) 新製品を宣伝すること
(B) 文書を破棄すること
(C) 古い電化製品を再利用すること
(D) 慈善団体への資金を集めること

16. 手伝いを申し出ると、聞き手たちは何をもらいますか。

(A) コーヒー用マグカップ
(B) ラッフルくじの抽選券
(C) 賞与の支払い
(D) 1 日の休暇

Questions 17 through 19 refer to the following announcement and table.

問題 17-19 は次のお知らせと表に関するものです。

M Good morning! It looks like everyone's on the bus now. Did you enjoy your breakfast? We wanted to give you a sampling of traditional, regional specialties specific to South India. OK, we have a long day of activities ahead! Due to heavy rain last night, unfortunately, the forest trek's been canceled — the trails are too muddy. But the other events are still on. I'm looking forward to leading your rafting adventure, and I know the other guides are excited to share their activities!

おはようございます！このバスに皆さんご乗車のようですね。朝食はお楽しみいただけましたか。皆さんに南インドならではの伝統的な郷土料理をお試しいただきたかったのです。さて、今日はいろいろなアクティビティーが待っている長い一日ですよ！昨夜の大雨のせいで、残念ながら森林トレッキングは中止となりました──山道がひどくぬかるんでいますので。ですが、他のイベントは予定通りです。私は皆さんを急流下りにお連れするのが楽しみですし、他のガイドたちも自分たちのアクティビティーにご案内することにわくわくしていますよ！

アクティビティー	ガイド
森林散策	Kavi Gupta
市場見学	Vinod Prasad
急流下り	Anil Krishnan
野生動物保護区	Rohan Singh

17. 話し手は聞き手たちの朝食について何と言っていますか。

(A) 地元の伝統的な食べ物が含まれていた。
(B) プロのシェフによって準備された。
(C) 健康的な食材で作られた。
(D) ビュッフェ形式で提供された。

18. なぜ、あるアクティビティーが中止になりましたか。

(A) 公園が早く閉まるから
(B) ガイドが対応できないから
(C) 十分な数の人々が申し込まなかったから
(D) 野外の状況が不向きだから

19. 図を見てください。話し手は誰ですか。

(A) Kavi Gupta
(B) Vinod Prasad
(C) Anil Krishnan
(D) Rohan Singh

Section 3 正解／スクリプト／訳

正解一覧

Part 1	**1** (C)					
Part 2	**2** (A)	**3** (B)	**4** (A)	**5** (B)	**6** (C)	**7** (B)
Part 3	**8** (A)	**9** (C)	**10** (B)	**11** (D)	**12** (B)	**13** (B)
Part 4	**14** (C)	**15** (C)	**16** (A)	**17** (C)	**18** (D)	**19** (B)

Part 1

1. Look at the picture marked number 1 in your test book.
問題用紙の 1 の写真を見てください。

W
(A) He's hanging some items on a rack. 彼は棚に物をつるしているところである。
(B) He's wiping a countertop. 彼は調理台を拭いている。
(C) He's using a scale. 彼ははかりを使っている。
(D) He's pressing a button on a telephone. 彼は電話のボタンを押している。

Part 2

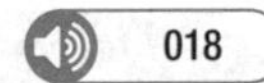

2. M When is that new French restaurant opening? あの新しいフランス料理店はいつオープンしますか。

M (A) Next Friday. 次の金曜日です。
(B) Turn left at the corner. 角を左に曲がってください。
(C) No, I took Spanish. いいえ、私はスペイン語を履修しました。

3. W We stack the chairs over there, right? あそこに椅子を積み重ねるんですよね?

M (A) I took the stairs instead. 私は代わりに階段を使いました。
(B) Yes, thanks for your help. はい、手伝ってくれてありがとう。
(C) I'll attend the banquet. 私は宴会に出席する予定です。

4. W Who's in charge of organizing the fund-raiser? 誰が資金集めイベントの企画を担当していますか。

M (A) Hiroko, as far as I know. 私の知る限りでは、Hiroko です。
(B) Yes, it is fun. はい、楽しいです。
(C) These books are organized well. これらの本はきちんと整理されています。

5. M How many sandwiches should I order for the client luncheon? 顧客との昼食会用にサンドイッチを幾つ注文すればいいですか。

W (A) Yes, that's right. はい、その通りです。
(B) At least twenty. 少なくとも 20 個です。
(C) In the conference room. 会議室内です。

6. M Which team is designing the electric car model? どのチームがその電気自動車のモデルを設計していますか。

W (A) Most of the workers get here by bus. 従業員のほとんどはここにバスで来ます。
(B) They're still standing in a line. 彼らはまだ列に並んでいます。
(C) There's a new team in Hong Kong. 香港に新しいチームがあります。

7. W I just put contracts for you to sign in your mailbox. ちょうど今、署名していただく契約書をあなたの郵便受けに入れました。

M (A) No, you take a right at the stop sign. いいえ、一時停止の標識のところで右折です。
(B) I'm leaving now for a business trip. 私は今から出張に出かけるところなのです。
(C) Yes, the chairs should arrive tomorrow. はい、椅子は明日届くはずです。

Part 3

019

Questions 8 through 10 refer to the following conversation.

問題 8-10 は次の会話に関するものです。

M Ingrid, I just had a chance to review the résumés you'd selected for the accounting position.

Ingrid、会計職の候補にあなたが選び出した履歴書を先ほど精査してみました。

W What are your thoughts about the pool of candidates?

候補者グループについてどう思いますか。

M Some promising people in the mix, but Hans Weber's résumé stood out the most to me. It's clear that he'd bring a vast amount of accounting experience to the table.

さまざまいる中で見込みある人が何人か混ざっていますが、Hans Weber の履歴書が一番私の目を引きました。彼が会計処理の極めて豊富な経験を発揮するであろうことは明らかです。

W I'm with you. He's spent nearly two decades in the field. You know, Martina should weigh in on the decision, since she's the director of our department. Let me check her schedule to see when she's free.

同感です。彼は 20 年近くこの分野で働いています。思ったのですが、Martina もこの判断に加わるべきですよね、彼女が当部署の統括者ですから。いつ時間があるか彼女のスケジュールを確認しますよ。

8. 話し手たちは主に何について話し合っていますか。

(A) 採用の決定
(B) 研修の機会
(C) 退職祝い
(D) 会計監査

9. 男性は Hans Weber について何を強調していますか。

(A) 最近、賞を獲得した。
(B) 優れた組織力がある。
(C) 経験が豊富である。
(D) チームでうまく協力して働く。

10. 女性は何をすると言っていますか。

(A) 報告書を書く
(B) 同僚の空き時間を確認する
(C) 会社の発表を準備する
(D) 会場を確認する

Questions 11 through 13 refer to the following conversation.

問題 11-13 は次の会話に関するものです。

W Santiago, we're having the research team meeting soon, right? To finalize the budget proposal?

Santiago、もうすぐ研究チーム会議がありますよね? 予算案を仕上げるためですね?

M Yes, we're almost done. We just have to figure out how many research interns we'll hire for next year. Not everyone on the team agrees on the number.

そうです、もう少しでできます。あとは来年、研究員のインターンを何人雇うか決める必要があるだけです。チーム全員が人数について合意しているわけではありませんので。

W Well, the budget's due by five o'clock.

ええと、予算の提出期限は 5 時までですよ。

M We should be able to meet the deadline.

期限に間に合わせられるはずです。

W Actually, I have to meet a client right after our meeting, so I can't send the final copy to the director.

実は、私は会議のすぐ後に顧客に会わなければならないので、最終案を部長に送信できません。

M Don't worry. I'll make sure she gets it.

ご心配なく。私が必ず彼女がそれを受け取るようにします。

11. 話し手たちはどの部署で働いていると思われますか。

(A) 人事
(B) 販売
(C) 経理
(D) 研究

12. 会議では何が話し合われますか。

(A) どのくらいの時間をプロジェクトに費やすべきか
(B) 何人のインターンを採用すべきか
(C) いつ製品を売り出すべきか
(D) 誰が実績評価を完成させるべきか

13. 女性はなぜ "I can't send the final copy to the director" と言っていますか。

(A) 自分の経験不足を謝罪するため
(B) 男性の手助けを求めるため
(C) 見直し用の草案送付を提案するため
(D) 承認プロセスを明確にするため

Part 4

021

Questions 14 through 16 refer to the following talk.

M In today's workshop, you'll learn how to use some graphic design software. I've selected the particular software we're using today because it doesn't require advanced drawing skills. So it's great for people just starting to learn. You'll be practicing by making event invitations. So if you're planning a party, you'll be able to create customized invitations for that today. Keep in mind, however, that we only have two hours, so you may not be able to finish. If that happens, come speak with me later, and you can sign up for some extra time in the lab for free.

問題 14-16 は次の話に関するものです。

本日の講習会では、グラフィックデザインのソフトウエアの使い方を学びます。私が本日使うこの特定のソフトウエアを選んだ理由は、高度な描画スキルを必要としないためです。ですから、これは勉強を始めたばかりの人たちにぴったりです。皆さんにはイベント招待状作りで練習してもらいます。ですので、もしパーティーを計画しているなら、そのための特製の招待状を今日作れるようになりますよ。ただ、心に留めておいていただきたいのですが、時間が 2 時間しかないので、最後まで仕上げられないかもしれません。そうなった場合は、後で私に声を掛けていただければ、無料で教室使用の時間延長を申し込むことができます。

14. 話し手はなぜあるソフトウエアを選んだのですか。

(A) 自分の会社で作られたものである。
(B) モバイル端末と互換性がある。
(C) 初心者に適している。
(D) 低価格である。

15. 聞き手たちは今日の講習会で何を作りますか。

(A) 店の看板
(B) 製品のラベル
(C) イベントの招待状
(D) 雑誌の表紙

16. 話し手によると、聞き手たちは後で何ができますか。

(A) 追加時間を申し込む
(B) 支払いをする
(C) 講座のカタログを要望する
(D) 取扱説明書を手に入れる

Questions 17 through 19 refer to the following excerpt from a meeting and benefits summary.

問題 17-19 は次の会議の一部と給付の概要に関するものです。

W As you know, trucking businesses like ours are facing a severe driver shortage. If we're going to keep up with our clients' shipping demands, then we need to hire at least three new drivers by the end of next month. So, the purpose of this management meeting is to look at how we can attract new recruits. Our, um, current benefits package for new drivers is outlined on the paper in front of you. I suggest we start by raising the sign-on bonus. Since it's a one-time hiring bonus, it'll cost less over time.

ご承知の通り、当社のようなトラック運送企業は深刻なドライバー不足に直面しています。顧客の配送需要に遅れずに対応していくつもりなら、来月末までに少なくとも3人のドライバーを新たに雇う必要があります。そこで、この経営会議の目的は、どうすれば新入社員を引き付けることができるかを検討することです。当社の、ええと、新規のドライバーに対する現在の諸給付の概要がお手元の資料に記されています。入社一時金の引き上げから始めてみてはどうでしょう。1度だけの雇用ボーナスなので、長い目で見れば安上がりになります。

従業員給付	
1. 基本週給	1,300ドル
2. 入社一時金	5,000ドル
3. 休暇日数	10日
4. 私用休暇日数	5日

17. 話し手はどの業界で働いていると思われますか。

(A) エネルギー
(B) 観光
(C) 輸送
(D) 金融

18. 主にどんな問題が議論されていますか。

(A) 売り上げ不振
(B) 旧式の設備
(C) 予算削減
(D) 従業員不足

19. 図を見てください。話し手はどの給付の変更を勧めていますか。

(A) 給付1
(B) 給付2
(C) 給付3
(D) 給付4

Section 4 正解／スクリプト／訳

正解一覧

Part 1	**1** (B)					
Part 2	**2** (C)	**3** (B)	**4** (A)	**5** (C)	**6** (B)	**7** (A)
Part 3	**8** (A)	**9** (D)	**10** (B)	**11** (C)	**12** (D)	**13** (C)
Part 4	**14** (A)	**15** (D)	**16** (C)	**17** (B)	**18** (C)	**19** (B)

Part 1

1. Look at the picture marked number 1 in your test book.
問題用紙の 1 の写真を見てください。

W
(A) Some plates are being washed.
皿が洗浄されているところである。

(B) One of the women is holding some dishes.
女性の 1 人は数枚の皿を手に持っている。

(C) The women are filling a basket with food.
女性たちはかごを食べ物で満たしている。

(D) Some utensils are being dried.
食器類が乾燥されているところである。

Part 2

2. M Where can I buy tickets to the show? 公演のチケットはどこで買えますか。

M (A) Could you show me the manual? 説明書を見せていただけますか。
(B) About ten euros. 約 10 ユーロです。
(C) On our Web site. 当社ウェブサイト上です。

3. W Is your sales meeting this afternoon or tomorrow morning? あなた方の営業会議は今日の午後ですか、それとも明日の午前中ですか。

W (A) Some potential customers. 顧客になってくれそうな人たちです。
(B) It'll be tomorrow. 明日になるでしょう。
(C) Yes, that's right. はい、その通りです。

4. M Could you help plan the award ceremony? 授賞式の計画を立てるのを手伝ってもらえますか。

W (A) Sure, I'd love to. もちろん、喜んで。
(B) He couldn't find any. 彼は何も見つけられませんでした。
(C) A printing error. 印刷エラーです。

5. W We still need to update the store hours on our sign, don't we? あとまだ看板の営業時間を新しくしないといけませんよね?

M (A) These uniforms look nicer. この制服の方が見た目がいいです。
(B) I'd say it's at least ten miles. 私が思うに、少なくとも 10 マイルです。
(C) No, I did it already. いいえ、私がもうやりました。

6. W How do you feel about the phone company increasing its rates? 電話会社が料金を引き上げるという話をどう思いますか。

M (A) Sure, I'll add them to the list. もちろん、それらをリストに追加しておきます。
(B) I'm pretty sure that was just a rumor. まず間違いなくあれは単なるうわさだったのでしょう。
(C) That password changes every month. そのパスワードは毎月変わります。

7. M Can I borrow your laptop charger? ノートパソコンの充電器を借りてもいいですか。

W (A) Could you ask Enrique instead? 代わりに Enrique に頼んでもらえますか。
(B) There's an extra charge on our bill. 請求書に追加料金が記載されています。
(C) I forgot to make a reservation. 予約するのを忘れました。

Part 3

Questions 8 through 10 refer to the following conversation with three speakers.

問題 8-10 は 3 人の話し手による次の会話に関するものです。

W Welcome to the employment fair! Thank you both for visiting my table. Jenkins Freight is the biggest company at the local harbor. Our ships deliver goods all around the world.

就職説明会へようこそ！お二人とも、私のテーブルにお越しいただきありがとうございます。Jenkins 貨物社は地元の港で最大手の会社です。当社の船は世界中に商品を届けています。

M1 My friend and I are interested in a job loading ships at the harbor. But we both have the same concern.

友人と私は港で船に荷積みをする仕事に興味があります。ただ、2 人とも同じ心配があるんです。

M2 That's right. We noticed that Jenkins Freight is located pretty far from the nearest bus stop, and neither of us owns a car.

そうなんです。Jenkins 貨物社は最寄りのバス停からかなり離れた場所にあることに気付いたのですが、私たちはどちらも車を持っていないのです。

W Actually, since many of our employees use public transportation, the company created a free shuttle to and from the work site.

実は、当社従業員の多くが公共交通機関を利用しているため、会社は職場の行き帰り用の無料送迎バスを設けました。

M2 OK. I'll take an application then.

分かりました。それなら、応募用紙を頂きます。

W Wonderful. And here's a business card for each of you with my contact information.

よかったです。それから、私の連絡先入りの名刺もどうぞそれぞれお持ちください。

8. 女性はどんな種類の事業で働いていると思われますか。

(A) 海運会社
(B) 造船所
(C) 自動車整備士
(D) 釣りツアー事業者

9. 男性たちは何について心配していますか。

(A) 日程
(B) 注文手順
(C) 安全性の問題に関する研修
(D) 職場への交通手段

10. 女性は男性たちに何を渡していますか。

(A) 価格表の冊子
(B) 名刺
(C) 印刷した説明書
(D) 写真

Questions 11 through 13 refer to the following conversation.

問題 11-13 は次の会話に関するものです。

M Ji-Min, I'd like to discuss some building plans with you.

Ji-Min、設計プランについて話し合いたいのですが。

W Hi, Ravi. You're working on designing a visitor center for the city, right?

こんにちは、Ravi。あなたは市の案内所の設計に取り組んでいるんですよね?

M Yes. The client wants an entryway that gives a sense of the city's industrial past. I'm not sure my design accomplishes that.

はい。クライアントは市の産業の歴史を感じさせるような入り口通路を希望しています。私の設計がそれを実現できているかどうか自信がないのです。

W Do you want to show me the plans?

私に設計プランを見せてもらえますか。

M Haven't you seen them? I e-mailed them to you yesterday.

まだ見ていないのですね。昨日、E メールで送ったのですが。

W Oh. I've been having computer problems. But a technician is looking into it now.

ああ。ずっと私のパソコンの調子が悪くて。でも技術者が調べてくれているところです。

M That's good. I'll be interested to get your opinion.

それはよかった。あなたの意見をお聞きしたいです。

11. 話し手たちはどこで働いていると思われますか。

(A) 会計事務所
(B) 旅行代理店
(C) 建築事務所
(D) ソフトウエア会社

12. 男性は何について自信がないのですか。

(A) 納期に間に合わせること
(B) 支払いをすること
(C) 契約書を改訂すること
(D) クライアントの要望を満たすこと

13. 女性はなぜ "I've been having computer problems" と言っていますか。

(A) 新しいオフィス機器購入の正当性を説明するため
(B) 技術的な問題を抱えた同僚に支援を申し出るため
(C) 書類に目を通していないことを釈明するため
(D) 改定された会社方針を批判するため

Part 4

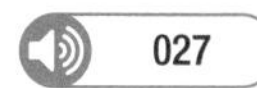

Questions 14 through 16 refer to the following announcement.

問題 14-16 は次のお知らせに関するものです。

W Attention, Cloudlake Gardens visitors! This is a reminder that the gardens will be closing early today for a private event at three P.M. For those attending the event, please make sure that you have your invitation with you. You'll need it to enter the reception area. To compensate for the early closure, parking fees have been waived for all visitors today. Thank you for your continued support for Cloudlake Gardens!

Cloudlake 庭園にご来園の皆さまにお知らせです！本日、当庭園は午後 3 時からの貸し切りイベントのため、早めに閉園となりますことを改めてお知らせいたします。このイベントに参加される方は、必ず招待状をお持ちください。受付にご入場の際にそれが必要になります。早めに閉園となるおわびといたしまして、本日ご来園の皆さま全員、駐車料金を不要とさせていただきます。日頃より Cloudlake 庭園をご愛顧いただきましてありがとうございます！

14. お知らせは主に何についてですか。

(A) 早めの閉園
(B) ボランティアの機会
(C) 音楽祭
(D) 寄付のお願い

15. 話し手は受付について何と言っていますか。

(A) 湖のすぐ横にある。
(B) 工事中である。
(C) 大人数の団体に対応できる。
(D) 入場には招待状が必要である。

16. 話し手は、今日は何が無料だと言っていますか。

(A) ガイド付きツアー
(B) 映画の上映会
(C) 駐車
(D) ポスター

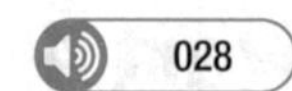

Questions 17 through 19 refer to the following telephone message and map.

問題 17-19 は次の電話のメッセージと地図に関するものです。

M Hello, I'm calling from Turnerville Landscaping Services. I inspected the trees on your company's property this morning as scheduled. You'll be happy to know that they're all very healthy — even the older ones near the pond. However, I'm worried about the trees growing along the road leading to the parking garage, because they have several low-hanging branches. For safety reasons, you should have those trees trimmed. I've prepared an estimate for the cost of the trimming work, which I'll e-mail to you shortly. If my proposal is acceptable to you, please call me back to make the necessary arrangements.

もしもし、Turnerville 造園サービスからお電話しています。今朝、予定通りに御社敷地内にある樹木を点検いたしました。樹木が全てとても健康だとお知りになれば、うれしく思われることでしょう――池の近くにある老齢の木もです。しかし、私は駐車場ビルにつながる道沿いに生えている木々のことを心配しています。というのも、何本かの枝が低く垂れ下がっているからです。安全上の理由から、あそこの木々は剪定した方がいいと思います。剪定作業費のお見積もりを用意いたしましたので、この後すぐEメールでお送りします。私の提案をご了承いただけましたら、必要な準備を進めますので折り返しお電話ください。

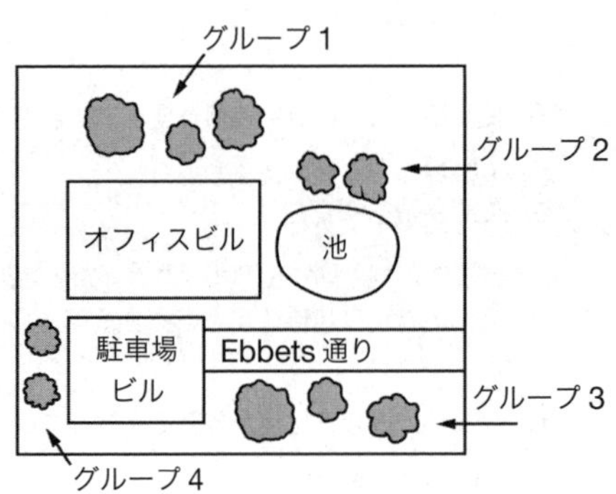

17. 電話の主な目的は何ですか。

(A) 作業が完了しなかった理由を説明すること
(B) 点検について最新情報を伝えること
(C) 園芸用品店に行くことを提案すること
(D) 人事異動を報告すること

18. 図を見てください。話し手はどのグループの木のことを気にしていますか。

(A) グループ 1
(B) グループ 2
(C) グループ 3
(D) グループ 4

19. 話し手は何を送ると言っていますか。

(A) 写真
(B) 費用見積もり
(C) 木の品種一覧
(D) 会社のパンフレット

Section 5 正解／スクリプト／訳

正解一覧

Part 1	1 (A)					
Part 2	2 (C)	3 (A)	4 (B)	5 (B)	6 (A)	7 (C)
Part 3	8 (C)	9 (A)	10 (D)	11 (B)	12 (D)	13 (C)
Part 4	14 (A)	15 (B)	16 (D)	17 (D)	18 (B)	19 (D)

Part 1

1. Look at the picture marked number 1 in your test book.
問題用紙の 1 の写真を見てください。

 W

(A) One of the people is standing near a staircase.
人々のうちの 1 人は階段の近くに立っている。

(B) One of the people is holding a plant.
人々のうちの 1 人は植物を手に持っている。

(C) One of the people is reading a sign.
人々のうちの 1 人は貼り紙を読んでいる。

(D) One of the people is unzipping a jacket.
人々のうちの 1 人は上着のファスナーを下ろしているところである。

Part 2

2. W Did the managers approve the budget proposal? 経営陣は予算案を承認しましたか。

M
(A) Time management. 時間管理です。
(B) Travel receipts. 旅費の領収書です。
(C) No, not yet. いいえ、まだです。

3. M Where do we store the office supplies? 事務用品をどこに保管していますか。

W
(A) In the back room. 奥の部屋です。
(B) A monthly purchase. 月1回の購入です。
(C) The store recently opened. その店は最近オープンしました。

4. W When will my dry cleaning be ready to pick up? 私のクリーニング品は、いつ引き取れるようになりますか。

M
(A) A cleaning supply company. 清掃用品の会社です。
(B) By Tuesday at noon. 火曜日の正午までには。
(C) Pass me the salt, please. 塩を取ってもらえますか。

5. M You received Jin-Ho's e-mail, didn't you? Jin-Ho の E メールを受け取りましたよね?

W
(A) The central post office. 中央郵便局です。
(B) Yes, I read it this morning. はい、今朝それを読みました。
(C) Because of the weather. 天気のせいです。

6. M This photography exhibition is very impressive. この写真展は大変見事ですね。

W
(A) Would you like to meet the organizer? 主催者にお会いになりたいですか。
(B) Black and white or color. 白黒またはカラーです。
(C) To the camera store. カメラ店へ。

7. W What's our strategy for increasing sales in the northern region? 北部地域で売り上げを伸ばすための当社の戦略は何ですか。

M
(A) I bought this coat at a 50 percent discount. 私はこのコートを 50 パーセント引きで買いました。
(B) The B train goes north, I think. B 列車は北行きだと思います。
(C) The strategy will be to use social media. 戦略はソーシャルメディアの活用になるでしょう。

Part 3

Questions 8 through 10 refer to the following conversation.

問題 8-10 は次の会話に関するものです。

W Omar, I wanted to talk to you about your proposal to start using recycled materials to make our printer paper.

Omar、当社のプリンター用紙の製造に再生材を使い始めたいというあなたの提案について話したかったんです。

M Yes. Research has shown that it's better for the environment to use recycled materials than to use wood from trees.

はい。研究では、再生材を使う方が樹木から採った木材を使うより環境に良いことが示されています。

W I see. But wouldn't it take longer to produce paper this way? I'm concerned that this change would cause major delays in production.

なるほど。しかし、その方法で紙を生産すると、今より時間がかかるのではないですか。私はこの変更によって生産に大きな遅れが生じるのではないかと懸念しています。

M Well, it's possible. But I think in the long term, our sales will increase because studies show consumers prefer to buy products made from recycled materials.

そうですね、その可能性はあります。しかし、長い目で見れば、当社の売り上げは伸びるでしょう。というのも、調査によれば、消費者は再生材で作られた製品を買う方を好むからです。

8. 話し手たちは何について話し合っていますか。

(A) 備品配達の予定を立てること
(B) 臨時職員を雇うこと
(C) 再生材を使うこと
(D) 設備を移動させること

9. 女性は何を懸念していますか。

(A) 生産の遅れ
(B) 予算の制約
(C) 製品の品質低下
(D) 安全規制

10. 男性は変更によって何が生じるだろうと言っていますか。

(A) エネルギー効率が向上する。
(B) 従業員がより満足する。
(C) 新製品が生み出される。
(D) 売り上げが伸びる。

Section 5

032

Questions 11 through 13 refer to the following conversation.

M Karima, the factory just received an order from State General Hospital. They're adding a second wing to their x-ray imaging center… they want to install 30 more x-ray machines, and they want our KAZ-2000 model.

W That's a big order! When does the hospital need the machines by?

M May first. We have some of the machines in stock, but your team will have to build at least 10 more… I can assign some extra people to help do this, if you think that's necessary.

W They don't take very long to build. I'll let you know if there are any problems.

問題 11-13 は次の会話に関するものです。

Karima、工場が先ほど州立総合病院から注文を受けました。X 線画像診断センターに第 2 病棟を増築するとのことです…レントゲン撮影機をもう 30 台設置したいそうで、先方は当社の KAZ-2000 モデルを要望しています。

それは大口の注文ですね！病院はいつまでに機械が必要なのですか。

5 月 1 日です。同機の在庫は何台かありますが、あなたのチームで少なくともあと 10 台は作らなければならないでしょう…もし必要そうなら、何人か追加の人員をこの手伝いに割り当てることができますよ。

あれの製造にはそれほど時間はかかりません。問題があればお知らせします。

11. 工場は何を作っていると思われますか。

(A) 個人用電化製品
(B) 医療機器
(C) 台所用家電
(D) エンジン部品

12. 女性は男性に何について尋ねていますか。

(A) プロジェクトの費用
(B) 製品検査の結果
(C) 新しい機械の所在
(D) 注文の納期

13. 女性はなぜ "They don't take very long to build" と言っていますか。

(A) プロジェクトが完了していないことに驚きを表すため
(B) すでに在庫としてある製品の使用を提案するため
(C) 追加の手伝いの申し出を断るため
(D) 製造工程への満足を表明するため

Part 4

Questions 14 through 16 refer to the following broadcast.

問題 14-16 は次の放送に関するものです。

M Welcome back to Channel 11 News! The city has accepted over 50 mural designs from local high school students. The winning school will receive money from participating local businesses to expand its arts programs. The winning mural will be painted on Downing Street in the city's shopping district. The mayor hopes it will draw more customers to the area. The city is asking for your help in selecting the best mural. Just go to the city's Web site and vote for your favorite.

再びチャンネル 11 ニュースへようこそ！ 市は地元の高校生からの 50 点を超える壁画のデザインを受け付けました。受賞した学校は地元の参加企業から、自校のアートプログラムを拡充するための賞金を受け取ることになります。受賞した壁画は市の商店街にある Downing 通りに描かれる予定です。市長は、この壁画が同地域により多くのお客を引き付けることを期待しています。市は最優秀の壁画を選定するに当たり、皆さんのご協力を求めています。市のウェブサイトにアクセスして、あなたのお気に入りの作品に投票してください。

14. 誰が市のコンテストに応募していますか。

(A) 高校生
(B) 美術館の館長
(C) 有名アーティスト
(D) 公務員

15. 受賞した壁画はどこに描かれますか。

(A) 川沿いの地域
(B) 商店街
(C) 公共公園
(D) 校庭

16. 聞き手たちは何をすることを勧められていますか。

(A) 欠員のある職に応募する
(B) 画材を寄付する
(C) アーティストと話す
(D) 受賞者を選ぶ手伝いをする

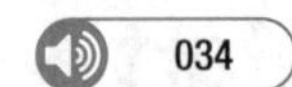

Questions 17 through 19 refer to the following telephone message and list.

W Hi, this is a message for Flower Bakery. This is Sakshi Gupta calling. I'm so sorry, I just looked at the clock and realized I'm behind schedule. I was supposed to come pick up my order today at one o'clock, and it's already past two. I just moved into a new apartment last week, and I've been so busy unpacking all my boxes that I totally forgot about my weekly bakery order! I can head over now, though. I'll be there shortly.

問題 17-19 は次の電話のメッセージと一覧表に関するものです。

もしもし、これは Flower ベーカリーさん宛てのメッセージです。こちらは Sakshi Gupta です。申し訳ありません、今ちょうど時計を見て、約束の時間に遅れていることに気付きました。今日 1 時に注文品を取りに伺うことになっていましたが、もう 2 時を過ぎています。私は先週新しいアパートに引っ越してきたところで、ずっと荷ほどきにかかりっきりで、毎週のパンの注文のことをすっかり忘れていました！でも今から向かえます。すぐにそちらに着きます。

日付：4 月 25 日		
Satoshi Ito	バニラケーキ 3 個	午前 9:00
Sakshi Gupta	パン 2 斤	午後 1:00
Maryam Rashad	クッキー 1 袋	午後 4:00
Felipe Reyes	ペストリー 24 個	午後 6:30

17. 電話の目的は何ですか。

(A) 割引について問い合わせること
(B) サービスについて苦情を言うこと
(C) 配達の予約を入れること
(D) 遅れた理由を説明すること

18. 図を見てください。話し手は何を注文しましたか。

(A) ケーキ
(B) パン
(C) クッキー
(D) ペストリー

19. 話し手は先週、何をしましたか。

(A) パーティーを開いた。
(B) 卒業式に出席した。
(C) 休暇に出掛けた。
(D) 新しいアパートに引っ越した。

Section 6 正解／スクリプト／訳

正解一覧

Part 1	1 (C)					
Part 2	2 (C)	3 (B)	4 (C)	5 (A)	6 (B)	7 (C)
Part 3	8 (C)	9 (C)	10 (D)	11 (B)	12 (A)	13 (C)
Part 4	14 (D)	15 (D)	16 (C)	17 (B)	18 (C)	19 (D)

Part 1

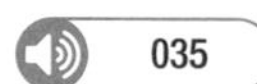

1. Look at the picture marked number 1 in your test book.
問題用紙の 1 の写真を見てください。

M
(A) An outdoor seating area is full of customers.
屋外の座席エリアが客でいっぱいである。

(B) A brick patio is under repair.
レンガ造りの中庭が修繕中である。

(C) The women are checking a mobile phone.
女性たちは携帯電話を確認している。

(D) The women are waiting near a checkout counter.
女性たちはレジの近くで待っている。

Part 2

2. W How can I purchase travel insurance?
旅行保険に加入するにはどうしたらいいですか。

W (A) A guided tour.
ガイド付きのツアーです。
(B) She bought a new purse.
彼女は新しい財布を買いました。
(C) I can help you with that.
それについては私がお手伝いできます。

3. W Why don't we plant more vegetables this year?
今年はもっと野菜を植えませんか。

M (A) Plenty of sunlight.
日当たり良好です。
(B) OK, that's a good idea.
そうですね、それはいい考えです。
(C) It's right over there.
ちょうどその先です。

4. M Just ask me if you have any questions about your job assignment.
業務の割り当てについて何か質問があれば、私に聞いてください。

W (A) Yes, I enjoyed it.
はい、私はそれを楽しみました。
(B) A customer questionnaire.
顧客アンケートです。
(C) Thanks, I probably will.
ありがとう、たぶんお聞きすると思います。

5. M Why is Ms. Chen picking up the materials for the new project?
Chen さんはなぜ新しいプロジェクトの資料を取りに来るのですか。

W (A) Because a manager has to sign for them.
責任者がそれに署名しなければならないからです。
(B) The projector is over there.
プロジェクターはあそこです。
(C) No, I haven't met her yet.
いいえ、私はまだ彼女に会っていません。

6. W My computer came with a five-year warranty, didn't it?
私のコンピューターは 5 年保証付きでしたよね?

M (A) I like historical novels.
私は歴史小説が好きです。
(B) Do you still have the original receipt?
領収書の原本をまだお持ちですか。
(C) He studies computer engineering.
彼はコンピューター工学を学んでいます。

7. M Maybe we should've left earlier.
私たちはもっと早く出発すべきだったかもしれません。

M (A) She's actually right-handed.
彼女は、本当は右利きです。
(B) No, I didn't leave anything behind.
いいえ、私は何も置き忘れませんでした。
(C) The meeting doesn't start for an hour.
会議はあと 1 時間は始まりませんよ。

Part 3

037

Questions 8 through 10 refer to the following conversation with three speakers.

問題 8-10 は 3 人の話し手による次の会話に関するものです。

M Hi, Anya. All the band's stage equipment has been loaded onto the truck, and I'm about to leave for the concert hall.

やあ、Anya。バンドのステージ機材は全部トラックに積み込んだので、これからコンサートホールに向かうところです。

W1 Actually, since you're new to the crew and haven't been to that venue before, I've asked Martina to go with you to show you where we need to park our truck. Oh, here she is. Martina, are you ready to go to the concert hall?

実のところ、あなたはこのチームに加わったばかりで前にあの会場に行ったことがないので、Martina にあなたと一緒に行って、どこにトラックを止める必要があるか教えてあげるように頼んであります。あっ、彼女が来ましたよ。Martina、もうコンサートホールに行けますか。

W2 Yes, I am. And by the way, we'll have some extra time to get the stage equipment set up there. I was just talking to the band about the sound check, and they said it's scheduled for six P.M., not five as we thought.

はい、大丈夫です。それはそうと、向こうでステージ機材を設置するのにちょっと時間の余裕ができそうです。ついさっきサウンドチェックについてバンドのメンバーと話していたのですが、午後 6 時の予定だと言っていました。私たちが思っていた 5 時ではなくて。

8. 話し手たちはどんな業界で働いていると思われますか。

(A) 観光
(B) 報道
(C) 音楽
(D) 映画

9. Martina は男性に何を教える予定ですか。

(A) 車両への荷物の積み込み方
(B) 車両の清掃の仕方
(C) 車両を駐車する場所
(D) 車両を取りに行く場所

10. Martina によると、何をするのに時間の余裕がありそうですか。

(A) 報告書を作成する
(B) 夕食を取る
(C) インタビューをする
(D) 機材を設置する

Section 6

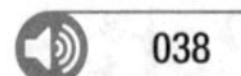

Questions 11 through 13 refer to the following conversation and map.

問題 11-13 は次の会話と地図に関するものです。

W　Hi, Greg. I just got to the Main Street Station. I'm calling to see if you're here yet.

もしもし、Greg。今、Main Street 駅に着きました。あなたがもう着いているか確かめるために電話しています。

M　Yes, I'm here. We've got plenty of time to meet the real estate agent who's going to show us the available office space. Our appointment isn't until three o'clock.

はい、着いていますよ。空き事務所を案内してくれる予定の不動産業者と会うまで時間はたっぷりあります。私たちの約束は 3 時からですので。

W　OK. Where should I meet you?

分かりました。どこであなたと会えばいいですか。

M　I'll wait for you at the exit closest to the ticket counter. Leaving from there will give us the shortest walk to the building we're going to.

切符売り場に一番近い出口であなたを待っています。そこから出発すれば、私たちが向かうビルまで最短距離で歩いて行けますよ。

W　And since we have a little extra time, let's stop and get a snack along the way.

それから、少し時間に余裕があるので、途中で立ち寄って軽食を買いましょう。

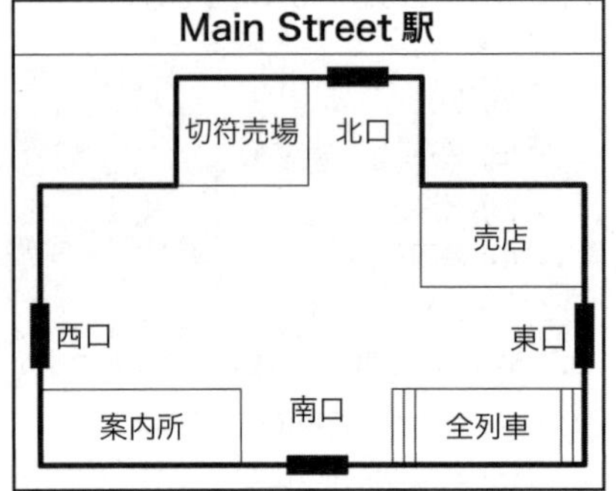

11. 話し手たちは 3 時に何をする予定ですか。

(A) 研修に参加する
(B) 事務所用スペースを見る
(C) 講習会を実施する
(D) 工場を検査する

12. 図を見てください。話し手たちはどの出口で会いますか。

(A) 北
(B) 東
(C) 南
(D) 西

13. 女性は何を提案していますか。

(A) 上司に電話すること
(B) 代金を送金すること
(C) 食べ物を買うこと
(D) もっと早い電車に乗ること

Part 4

039

Questions 14 through 16 refer to the following introduction.

M Thank you for attending this annual gathering for industry leaders in plastics manufacturing. Today, I'm pleased to introduce Zoya Petrova, chair of the Committee for Environmental Sustainability in Plastics. Her committee was formed eight years ago to focus on ways manufacturers can reduce the environmental impact of plastics production. Now there are 24 members! In a moment, Ms. Petrova will be presenting the steps of a plan that she's devised to help manufacturers transition to using more biodegradable plastics. The handout you received outlines these steps. Now join me in welcoming our guest speaker!

問題 14-16 は次の紹介に関するものです。

プラスチック製造業界をけん引する皆さまのためのこの年次集会にご出席いただき、ありがとうございます。本日は謹んで、プラスチック業界における環境的持続可能性委員会委員長 Zoya Petrova をご紹介申し上げます。彼女の委員会は、製造会社がプラスチック製造の環境への影響を軽減できる方法に重点的に取り組むことを目的として、8 年前に結成されました。現在、24 のメンバーがおります！この後すぐ、製造会社が生分解性プラスチックの使用増加へと移行する手助けをするためにご自身が考案された計画の各段階について、Petrova さんが発表してくださいます。お手元の配布資料にこれらの各段階の概要が記載してあります。では、ご一緒にゲストスピーカーをお迎えしましょう！

14. 聞き手たちはどんな業界で働いていますか。

(A) 林業
(B) 公衆衛生
(C) 建築
(D) 製造

15. 話し手は "Now there are 24 members" という発言で、何を示唆していますか。

(A) 就職説明会が成功した。
(B) 会議室が小さ過ぎる。
(C) 会費が変更される。
(D) 組織が成長している。

16. 配布資料にはどんな情報が載っていますか。

(A) 参加者一覧
(B) 地域の地図
(C) 計画の各段階
(D) 研究結果

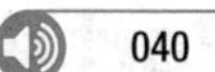

Questions 17 through 19 refer to the following excerpt from a meeting.

W Finally, a reminder that the company's transitioning to a different software that will allow us to connect our databases across the company. But since the current system works well, many of you have asked why we are making the change. Well, having a resource-planning system means that everyone, from the CEO to us in Accounting, can create, store, and use the same data. Please make sure you leave your laptops on your desk before heading out of the office on Friday. IT will be installing the new software over the weekend.

問題 17-19 は次の会議の一部に関するものです。

最後に、私たちが社内データベースを全社横断的に接続できるようにする別のソフトウエアに、当社が移行することを再度お知らせします。しかし、現行システムがうまく機能しているため、皆さんの多くからなぜ変更を行うのかという質問を頂きました。それについては、資源計画システムというものを持つことで、CEO から私たち経理部員まで全員が同じデータを作成・保存・使用することができるようになるわけです。金曜日の退社時は、必ずご自分のノートパソコンを机の上に置いたままにしてください。IT 部が週末の間に新しいソフトウエアをインストールする予定です。

17. 話し手は主に何について話していますか。

(A) 製造計画の修正
(B) 新しいソフトウエアシステム
(C) 会社の経営陣の変更
(D) 休暇方針の改定

18. 話し手によると、聞き手たちは何について尋ねましたか。

(A) 文書のパスワード
(B) 昇進の基準
(C) 決定の理由
(D) 社員研修の計画

19. 聞き手たちは金曜日に何をするべきですか。

(A) 業務スペースを掃除する
(B) チェックリストの記入を終える
(C) 取扱説明書をダウンロードする
(D) 機器を職場に置いていく

Section 7 正解／スクリプト／訳

正解一覧

Part 1	1 (C)					
Part 2	2 (B)	3 (A)	4 (C)	5 (A)	6 (C)	7 (B)
Part 3	8 (D)	9 (A)	10 (C)	11 (C)	12 (D)	13 (A)
Part 4	14 (C)	15 (B)	16 (D)	17 (A)	18 (D)	19 (A)

Part 1

1. Look at the picture marked number 1 in your test book.
問題用紙の 1 の写真を見てください。

M
(A) They're shaking hands. 彼女たちは握手をしている。
(B) They're exchanging business cards. 彼女たちは名刺を交換している。
(C) One of the women is receiving a booklet. 女性の 1 人は冊子を受け取っている。
(D) One of the women is searching through a filing cabinet. 女性の 1 人は書類整理棚の中を調べている。

Part 2

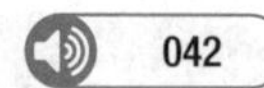

2. M Where is this tour going? / このツアーはどこに行くのですか。

W (A) From eight to noon. / 8時から正午までです。
(B) To all the popular attractions. / 人気の観光名所全てです。
(C) Yes, I'd like a ticket, please. / はい、チケットを1枚お願いします。

3. W Can I help you carry those notebooks? / それらのノートを運ぶのを手伝いましょうか。

M (A) I'd appreciate it. / それはありがたいです。
(B) Have you read it? / それを読みましたか。
(C) No, he just left. / いいえ、彼はたった今出発しました。

4. M The software is being updated this morning, isn't it? / ソフトウエアは今日の午前中に更新されるんですよね?

W (A) Be sure to wear it at all times. / 必ずそれを常時着用してください。
(B) It's just down the street. / その通りをちょっと行った所ですよ。
(C) No, not until after work hours. / いいえ、就業時間後までは更新されません。

5. M How many languages do you speak? / あなたは何カ国語を話せますか。

M (A) I'm fluent in two. / 2カ国語が流暢です。
(B) We haven't spoken to him. / 私たちは彼と話したことはありません。
(C) Mei Ting's trip to Italy. / Mei Tingのイタリア旅行です。

6. W Didn't they repair the air conditioner? / 彼らはエアコンを修理しなかったのですか。

M (A) A new pair of shoes. / 新しい靴です。
(B) He was promoted to a new position. / 彼は新しい役職に昇進しました。
(C) Yes, this morning. / しましたよ、今朝。

7. M Who's responsible for servicing these packaging machines? / これらの包装機の点検は誰が担当しているのですか。

W (A) Fifty bottles per minute. / 1分間にボトル50本です。
(B) I think Jang-Ho is. / Jang-Hoだと思います。
(C) The delivery schedule. / 納品日程です。

Part 3

043

Questions 8 through 10 refer to the following conversation.

問題 8-10 は次の会話に関するものです。

M Hi, Sunita. Do you have a minute?

お疲れさま、Sunita。少し時間がありますか。

W Yes, what's up?

はい、どうしましたか。

M I just got off the phone with Clarksdale Kitchen Supplies, a potential new client. They're considering having us manufacture a large order of food storage containers specifically for use in the home. Would you be able to set aside time to work on a few prototypes?

Clarksdale 台所用品社という新規見込み客との電話を先ほど切ったところです。先方は、家庭での使用に特化した食品保存容器の大量注文を当社に製造委託することを考えています。数点の試作品に取り組む時間を確保できそうですか。

W Sure. I'll need to know exactly what they're looking for, though. Product specifications — including color preferences, storage capacity, length and width measurements.

もちろんです。でも、私は先方が求めている物を正確に知る必要があります。製品の仕様——つまり、ご希望の色、保存容量、縦横のサイズなどです。

M Of course. Let me schedule a videoconference with the two of us and their representative so that we can go over all that. I'll set something up for this week.

確かにそうですね。そういったこと全てを検討できるよう、私たち 2 人と先方担当者とのビデオ会議の予定を組ませてください。今週中に何かしら設定します。

8. 話し合いは主に何についてですか。

(A) 雇用計画
(B) 資金要請
(C) 工程の刷新
(D) 試作品

9. 女性は何が必要だと言っていますか。

(A) 製品の仕様
(B) 収益予測
(C) 責任者の承認
(D) 最新の予定表

10. 男性は何をする計画を立てていますか。

(A) 参考資料を確認する
(B) 供給業者の入札を比較する
(C) ビデオ会議を手配する
(D) 取扱説明書を参照する

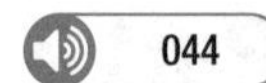

Questions 11 through 13 refer to the following conversation and coupon.

問題 11-13 は次の会話とクーポンに関するものです。

M Thanks for shopping with us today. Did you find everything you needed?

本日は当店でお買い物いただきまして、ありがとうございます。ご入用の物は全ておそろいですか。

W Yes, thank you. I just started a new job last month, and I'll be taking lots of business trips. I found this suitcase that will fit in the overhead compartment on an airplane. Oh, and I have this coupon.

はい、ありがとうございます。私は先月新しい仕事を始めたばかりで、出張が多くなりそうなんです。機内の頭上の荷物入れに収まるこのスーツケースを見つけました。あ、それから私はこのクーポンを持っています。

M Excellent. Regular price for the suitcase is 80 dollars, so you get a nice discount.

大変結構ですね。このスーツケースの通常価格は 80 ドルですので、かなりのお値引きを受けられますよ。

W I'm glad I have this coupon.

このクーポンがあってよかった。

M Here's your receipt. Don't forget to answer our survey online for a chance to win a gift card to our store.

こちらがレシートです。当店のギフトカードを獲得できるチャンスがありますので、私どものオンラインアンケートにお答えいただくのをお忘れなく。

Climson デパートクーポン券

10% 引き：25 ドル以下
15% 引き：26 ～ 50 ドル
20% 引き：51 ～ 75 ドル
25% 引き：76 ドル以上

購入額全額に対しての割引

11. 女性は先月、何をしたと言っていますか。

(A) 休暇に出掛けた。
(B) イベントを企画した。
(C) 新しい仕事を始めた。
(D) 新しい事業所を開いた。

12. 図を見てください。女性はどの割引を受けますか。

(A) 10 パーセント
(B) 15 パーセント
(C) 20 パーセント
(D) 25 パーセント

13. 女性はどうすればギフトカードを獲得できますか。

(A) アンケートに記入することによって
(B) コンテストに参加することによって
(C) 友人を紹介することによって
(D) 会報を申し込むことによって

Part 4

Questions 14 through 16 refer to the following talk.

W Welcome to Allnay Incorporated. My name's Soo-Min and I'll be helping you through your first day of employment here. First, I'm going to give you each an employee identification card, which you'll have to scan each time you enter the building. Make sure your name's spelled correctly on the front. If it's misspelled, we'll need to have a new card issued. Once I pass these out, you can take a five-minute break. After that, I'll show you around the building so that you know where everything is.

問題 14-16 は次の話に関するものです。

Allnay 社へようこそ。私の名前は Soo-Min で、入社初日を通して皆さんをサポートします。まず、皆さんそれぞれに従業員 ID カードをお渡ししますが、これは皆さんが建物に入るたびにスキャンしなければなりません。表側にご自分の名前が正しくつづられているか確認してください。もしつづりに誤りがあれば、新しいカードを発行してもらう必要があります。私がこれらを配布し終えたら、5 分間の休憩にしましょう。その後、皆さんにいろいろな物の場所を覚えていただけるよう、私が建物内をご案内します。

14. 話し手はそれぞれの聞き手に何を渡す予定ですか。

(A) 昼食券
(B) 推薦状
(C) ID カード
(D) 雇用契約書

15. 話し手は聞き手たちに何を確認するよう求めていますか。

(A) ロゴの色
(B) 名前のつづり
(C) 署名の日付
(D) 事務所の所在地

16. 休憩の後、聞き手たちは何をする予定ですか。

(A) 会社の制服を試着する
(B) E メールのアカウントにログインする
(C) 集合写真用にポーズをとる
(D) 建物内の見学に行く

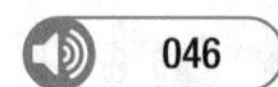

Questions 17 through 19 refer to the following telephone message.

W Mr. Watanabe, this is the operations manager at our plastics factory in Osaka. I'm calling to tell you that I've put in a work order to have one of the plastic molding machines serviced. It turns out that there was condensation buildup in the machine, which was causing defects. And the order for the Englewood Craft Company was supposed to go out today. It took three hours to discover the problem. This isn't the first time. Remember when production was stopped on several machines due to warping? There are software programs available that provide continuous monitoring for problems just like this. Can we discuss them at the next managers' meeting?

問題 17-19 は次の電話のメッセージに関するものです。

Watanabe さん、こちらは大阪のプラスチック工場の運用管理者です。プラスチック成形機 1 台を修理させる作業指示を出したことをお伝えするためにお電話しています。機械の中に結露が蓄積し、そのせいで不具合が生じていたことが分かっています。Englewood 工芸社の注文分は本日出荷するはずだったのですが。この問題を明らかにするのに 3 時間かかってしまいました。これは初めてではありません。ゆがみが原因で数台の機械で製造が停止したのを覚えていますか。まさに今回のような問題を継続的に監視するソフトウエアプログラムがあります。次の管理者会議でそれについて話し合えますか。

17. 話し手はどこで働いていますか。

(A) プラスチック製造工場
(B) 電子機器会社
(C) 建設会社
(D) 自動車修理店

18. 話し手はなぜ "It took three hours to discover the problem" と言っていますか。

(A) 配置転換を願い出るため
(B) 同僚について不満を訴えるため
(C) 残業手当を要求するため
(D) 出荷の遅れを説明するため

19. 話し手は今後の会議で何について話し合いたいと思っていますか。

(A) ソフトウエアプログラム
(B) 売上報告書
(C) 製品広告
(D) 採用の決定

Section 8 正解／スクリプト／訳

正解一覧

Part 1	1 (B)					
Part 2	2 (C)	3 (B)	4 (B)	5 (B)	6 (A)	7 (C)
Part 3	8 (B)	9 (A)	10 (D)	11 (B)	12 (C)	13 (B)
Part 4	14 (B)	15 (C)	16 (A)	17 (D)	18 (A)	19 (C)

Part 1

1. Look at the picture marked number 1 in your test book.
問題用紙の 1 の写真を見てください。

M
(A) Some dishes of food have been left under a window.
料理を盛り付けた皿が窓の下に残されている。

(B) Some decorations have been mounted on the wall.
装飾が壁に取り付けてある。

(C) Plates have been stacked by a windowsill.
皿が窓台のそばに積み重ねられている。

(D) Plants have been placed on the tables.
植物がテーブルの上に置かれている。

Part 2

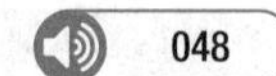

2. M Why isn't the moving van parked out front? なぜ引っ越し用小型トラックが表に止まっていないのですか。

W
(A) A two-bedroom apartment. 寝室が2つあるアパートです。
(B) Yes, the park is lovely today. はい、今日の公園はすてきですよ。
(C) I'll have to check with Hao Nan. Hao Nanに確認しなければなりませんね。

3. W Didn't she receive my message? 彼女は私のメッセージを受け取らなかったのですか。

M
(A) So nice to meet you. お会いできてとてもうれしいです。
(B) No, she's been on vacation. 受け取っていません、彼女は休暇中です。
(C) Yes, your receipt's in the bag. 受け取りました、あなたの領収証は袋の中です。

4. W Where's the training session being held? 研修会はどこで行われていますか。

M
(A) Let me hold that. 私がそれを持ちますよ。
(B) In the conference room. 会議室です。
(C) On Friday afternoon. 金曜の午後です。

5. M How deep will the foundation of the new building be? 新しい建物の基礎はどのくらいの深さになりますか。

W
(A) Bus 220 will drop you off right in front. 220番バスに乗れば、すぐ前で降ろしてくれます。
(B) I'm still waiting for the plans from the architect. まだ建築士の図面待ちです。
(C) Some shovels and other tools. スコップ数本と他の道具類です。

6. M Would you like to place an order today or wait until tomorrow? 本日注文されますか、それとも明日までお待ちになりますか。

W
(A) Tomorrow morning would be better. 明日の朝の方がよさそうです。
(B) Some printer ink and paper. プリンターのインクと紙です。
(C) No, they're not in alphabetical order. いいえ、それはアルファベット順になっていません。

7. M When can you meet with me to discuss the budget? いつ私と会って予算の相談をしてもらえますか。

W
(A) 215 Elm Street. Elm通り215番地です。
(B) To the office. 事務所へ。
(C) How about this afternoon? 今日の午後はどうですか。

Part 3

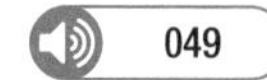

Questions 8 through 10 refer to the following conversation with three speakers.

問題 8-10 は 3 人の話し手による次の会話に関するものです。

M1 Our reservations for next summer during the championship cup haven't been keeping pace with the other resorts on the beach. Some of them are already fully booked.

来夏のチャンピオンズカップ期間中の当施設の予約は、ビーチの他のリゾート施設に後れを取っています。中にはすでに満室になっている所もありますよ。

W It's probably just because we're at the farthest end of the beach away from the stadium. Don't worry about it. All our rooms will be booked soon enough.

おそらく、単にうちがビーチの端でスタジアムから一番遠いからでしょう。心配しないでください。うちも間もなく全室が予約で埋まりますよ。

M1 What do you think, Thomas?

どう思いますか、Thomas。

M2 I agree with Hiroko. But if you're really concerned, we can add a few incentives to our all-inclusive packages to make them stand out. Scuba lessons, perhaps?

Hiroko と同意見です。でも、本当に心配なら、諸費用込みのパッケージプランに幾つか引きになるサービスを追加して目立たせるようにすればいいのでは。スキューバ教室とか?

M1 Maybe. I'll run some calculations and see what I can come up with.

そうかもしれませんね。ちょっと計算してみて、何が考えられるか検討してみます。

8. どんなイベントが次の夏に行われますか。

(A) 地方選挙
(B) スポーツ大会
(C) 展示会
(D) 祝祭日の祭り

9. 女性は何が問題の原因だと言っていますか。

(A) 事業の立地
(B) 交通費
(C) 天気予報の変更
(D) 講演者のキャンセル

10. Thomas はどんな提案をしていますか。

(A) コンサルタントを雇うこと
(B) イベントの日を変更すること
(C) テレビで宣伝を打つこと
(D) 追加の誘因となるものを提供すること

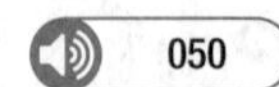

Questions 11 through 13 refer to the following conversation and directory.

問題 11-13 は次の会話と案内板に関するものです。

M Welcome to Burnham Medical Clinic, how can I help you?

Burnham 医療クリニックへようこそ、ご用件を承ります。

W Hi, I'm here to pick up my aunt. She's meeting with a fitness coach.

こんにちは、おばを迎えに来ました。おばは運動指導員の方と会っているところです。

M Oh, sure. But I'll need you to write down your name and the current time here in the visitor's log.

ああ、分かりました。ただ、こちらの来訪者記録にあなたのお名前と現在時刻を書いていただく必要があります。

W OK… that's done. And I'm a little early…

はい…済みました。それから私、少し早く来てしまったのですが…。

M Well, you're welcome to wait. There are plenty of chairs here in the lobby.

でしたら、どうぞお待ちになってください。このロビーには椅子がたくさんありますから。

診療所案内板

Emiko Sato、栄養士	104 号室
Salma Aziz、運動指導員	105 号室
Wu Zhang、理学療法士	106 号室
Anil Ortiz、健康相談員	107 号室

11. 図を見てください。女性のおばは誰と会っていますか。

(A) Emiko Sato
(B) Salma Aziz
(C) Wu Zhang
(D) Anil Ortiz

12. 男性は女性に何をするように頼んでいますか。

(A) 薬局に連絡する
(B) 予約を入れる
(C) 来訪者記録に名前を書く
(D) 身元証明書を提示する

13. 女性は次に何をすると思われますか。

(A) 駐車許可証をもらう
(B) ロビーで待つ
(C) 電話をかける
(D) 小冊子を読む

Part 4

051

Questions 14 through 16 refer to the following telephone message.

W This is Sameera Kapoor calling from Cityvale Savings and Loan. I'm reviewing the small-business loan application you submitted earlier this week. It looks like you have a good business plan, but, unfortunately, I cannot approve your loan at this time. As indicated on page three of the instructions, you need to provide the names of several references. Specifically, we want to speak with some associates who can vouch for your previous business dealings. I'd be happy to answer any questions. I work until five today.

問題 14-16 は次の電話のメッセージに関するものです。

Cityvale 貯蓄貸付組合の Sameera Kapoor がお電話しています。今週先立ってご提出いただいた小規模事業の資金融資申請を見直しているところです。良い事業計画をお持ちのようですが、残念ながら現時点では融資の承認をいたしかねます。説明資料の 3 ページにありますように、身元保証人数名のお名前をご提示いただく必要があります。具体的に言うと、当組合はあなたの過去の商取引を保証できるお仲間の方々とお話しさせていただきたいのです。どんなご質問にも喜んでお答えいたします。本日私は 5 時まで勤務しております。

14. 話し手はどのような分野で働いていますか。

(A) マーケティング
(B) 金融
(C) 不動産
(D) 人事

15. 話し手は何を要望していますか。

(A) 署名
(B) 写真
(C) 身元保証人のリスト
(D) 証明書の写し

16. 話し手はなぜ "I work until five today" と言っていますか。

(A) 都合がつく時間を示すため
(B) 招待を受けるため
(C) 助力を求めるため
(D) 誤解を正すため

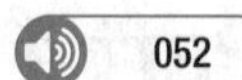

Questions 17 through 19 refer to the following excerpt from a meeting.

M My father started this pool equipment business many years ago, so this company's been around for quite a while. Of course, as times change, our approach does as well. So, to start off today's staff meeting, I'll be introducing our company's new products. We've decided to branch out and develop equipment specifically designed for aquatic exercise at fitness centers. I'm sure that some of you might have concerns that a new type of product could be risky. But you've all heard of the chain of fitness centers called Banner Fitness Centers, right? Well, they've already agreed to purchase our new aquatic equipment for all of their locations. And it's a large order!

問題 17-19 は次の会議の一部に関するものです。

私の父はこのプール器具の事業を何年も前に始めたので、この会社は長年事業を続けてきました。もちろん、時代が変わるとともに、私たちの取り組みも変わります。そこで、今日の社員会議を始めるに際し、当社の新製品をご紹介したいと思います。当社は商売の手を広げ、フィットネスセンターでの水中エクササイズ専用に設計された器具を開発することにしました。新しいタイプの製品はリスクを伴う可能性があると懸念する方もいるに違いありません。しかし、皆さん方全員が Banner フィットネスセンターというフィットネスチェーンのことを耳にされたことがありますよね？ 実は、同社がすでに当社の新しい水中器具を全店舗用に購入することに同意しています。そしてこれは大量注文です！

17. なぜ話し手は自分の父親に言及していますか。

(A) 新製品考案の功績が父親にあることを認めるため
(B) 退職祝賀会を告知するため
(C) 経営判断を疑問視するため
(D) 会社の長い歴史を強調するため

18. どんな種類の製品が説明されていますか。

(A) エクササイズ器具
(B) 掃除用品
(C) 健康的なスナック菓子
(D) 日曜大工道具

19. 話し手は "it's a large order" という発言で、何を意味していますか。

(A) 業務の手助けを求めている。
(B) 同僚の誤解を正している。
(C) ある製品ラインが成功すると確信している。
(D) 納期に間に合うかを懸念している。

Section 9 正解／スクリプト／訳

正解一覧

Part 1	1 (B)					
Part 2	2 (C)	3 (B)	4 (B)	5 (C)	6 (B)	7 (A)
Part 3	8 (B)	9 (C)	10 (B)	11 (C)	12 (A)	13 (B)
Part 4	14 (B)	15 (A)	16 (D)	17 (B)	18 (D)	19 (C)

Part 1

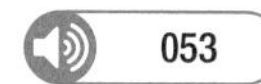

1. Look at the picture marked number 1 in your test book.
問題用紙の 1 の写真を見てください。

W (A) Some books are being removed from a table.
本がテーブルから片付けられている。

(B) Some of the chairs are not occupied.
椅子の幾つかは空いている。

(C) The man is sipping from a coffee cup.
男性はコーヒーカップから少しずつ飲んでいる。

(D) The woman is standing on a step stool.
女性は踏み台の上に立っている。

Part 2

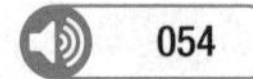

2. M When did that business open?
あの店はいつ開業したのですか。

W (A) The storage closet downstairs.
階下の収納室です。
(B) On Elmwood Avenue.
Elmwood 大通りです。
(C) About five years ago.
5 年ほど前です。

3. M Are you still working on the contract, or is this the final version?
契約書をまだ作成中ですか、それともこれが最終版ですか。

W (A) The television screen is working.
テレビ画面は正常に機能しています。
(B) I'm making one more change.
あと 1 カ所修正します。
(C) Thanks, it was a wonderful excursion.
ありがとう、素晴らしい小旅行でした。

4. M Why don't you join us for dinner?
私たちと一緒に夕食をいかがですか。

M (A) Yesterday, I think.
昨日だと思います。
(B) I'm sorry, but I can't.
あいにくですが、行けません。
(C) Can I borrow that book?
あの本をお借りしてもいいですか。

5. W How is Paul doing on the assembly line?
組立ラインで Paul はどんな様子ですか。

M (A) On the weekends.
週末にです。
(B) They ordered them online.
彼らはオンラインでそれらを注文しました。
(C) He still needs some supervision.
彼にはまだ少し監督が必要です。

6. W What did you think of the movie?
その映画をどう思いましたか。

W (A) A moving truck is coming tomorrow.
引っ越しのトラックは明日来ます。
(B) I didn't really like it.
私はあまり好きではありませんでした。
(C) Let's meet at the box office.
チケット売り場で待ち合わせしましょう。

7. M Don't you think it's time to have the printing machines serviced?
そろそろ印刷機を点検してもらう時期だと思いませんか。

M (A) It has been six months.
6 カ月たっていますからね。
(B) A three o'clock flight.
3 時のフライトです。
(C) Sure, I'll have a coffee.
はい、コーヒーを頂きます。

Part 3

Questions 8 through 10 refer to the following conversation.

問題 8-10 は次の会話に関するものです。

W Mario, we received a request from the McDonnell Marketing Firm to install digital screens in our trains. They're offering to install the screens at their expense. In exchange, they'd get some revenue from selling advertising space to third parties. How should I respond?

Mario、当社の電車にデジタルスクリーンを設置したいという McDonnell 市場調査社からの依頼を受けました。同社は先方費用負担でスクリーンを設置することを提案しています。それと引き換えに、同社は第三者に広告スペースを販売することで収益を得たいと考えています。どのように対応すればいいですか。

M Well, digital advertisements could be a big source of revenue for us. It really depends on how the firm plans to share the profits.

そうですね、デジタル広告は当社にとって大きな収入源になり得ます。実のところ、先方がどのように利益を分け合おうと考えているかによりますね。

W Another advantage is that we could use the screens to display transit maps, train times, and things like that.

もう 1 つの利点は、当社が路線図や発車時刻といったものを表示するのにスクリーンを使えそうなことですね。

M Good point, but we'd also have to negotiate for that in our agreement. Go ahead — set up a meeting with them. Let's hear their entire proposal.

いい指摘ですが、私たちは契約でそのことも取り決めなければならないでしょう。話を進めてください――先方との打ち合わせの設定をお願いします。先方の提案の全容を聞いてみましょう。

8. 話し手たちはどんな業界で働いていると思われますか。

(A) 情報技術
(B) 運輸
(C) 金融
(D) テレビ産業

9. 女性は提案のどんな利点について言及していますか。

(A) 幾つかの資材が地元で調達できる可能性がある。
(B) 幾つかの研修がオンラインに移行できる可能性がある。
(C) 幾つかの有益な情報を表示できる可能性がある。
(D) 幾つかのプロジェクト期間を短縮できる可能性がある。

10. 男性は女性に何をするよう頼んでいますか。

(A) 書式を印刷する
(B) 打ち合わせを設定する
(C) 契約書の草案を書く
(D) 決済を行う

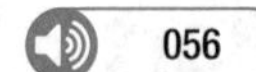

Questions 11 through 13 refer to the following conversation and price list.

問題 11-13 は次の会話と価格表に関するものです。

W Jackson Hardware Store, how can I help you?

Jackson 工具店です、どのようなご用件でしょうか。

M Hi. I'm assembling a bed I bought yesterday, but I don't have a tool I need.

こんにちは。昨日買ったベッドを組み立てているのですが、必要な工具がないのです。

W I'm sure I can help with that.

それについては間違いなくお役に立てます。

M Thanks. The instructions say that I need an adjustable wrench.

助かります。説明書に調整式レンチが必要とあります。

W Actually, we don't have any more of those in stock, but I know our Bloomington store has them. I can order one.

実は、当店にはもうその在庫がないのですが、Bloomington 店にはございます。私の方で注文いたしますよ。

M No, thanks. I don't live far from Bloomington, so I'll just go to that store.

いや、結構です。私の住まいは Bloomington から遠くないので、そちらの店に行くことにします。

価格表

商品	価格
調整式レンチ	3 ドル
1 メートル定規	5 ドル
ゴムハンマー	7 ドル
プラスドライバー	9 ドル

11. 男性は何に取り組んでいるところだと言っていますか。

(A) 機器の移動
(B) 部屋の塗装
(C) 家具の組み立て
(D) 電気器具の修理

12. 図を見てください。男性は工具に幾ら支払うことになりますか。

(A) 3 ドル
(B) 5 ドル
(C) 7 ドル
(D) 9 ドル

13. 女性は何をすると申し出ていますか。

(A) パスワードを確認する
(B) 商品を注文する
(C) 苦情を報告する
(D) 割引を適用する

Part 4

057

Questions 14 through 16 refer to the following excerpt from a meeting.

問題 14-16 は次の会議の一部に関するものです。

W OK, I have an update on an improvement to our Web site. As you know, online sales of our clothing line haven't been good. Customers have complained that the images were poor quality. To address this, we've recently made this aspect more interactive. Product images now appear three-dimensional: Customers can zoom in and rotate a picture of each clothing item. We plan to survey the first 100 customers who use the new feature to get some feedback. I'll share the results at our next meeting.

さて、当社のウェブサイトの改善に関する最新情報があります。ご存じのように、当社衣料品のオンラインでの売り上げは芳しくありません。お客さまから画像の質が良くないとの不満が出ています。これに対処するため、先日この点をよりインタラクティブにしました。現在は商品が3D画像で表示されます。お客さまがそれぞれの衣料品の写真を拡大したり回転させたりできるのです。この新機能を使用する最初の 100 名のお客さまにアンケートを取ってご意見を頂く計画です。次の会議で結果をお伝えします。

14. この会社は何を販売していますか。

(A) 家電製品
(B) 衣料品
(C) ソフトウエア
(D) 書籍

15. ウェブサイトのどんな機能が最近改善されましたか。

(A) どのように画像が表示されるか
(B) どれくらい速く購入できるか
(C) どのように商品詳細が書かれているか
(D) どれくらい簡単に商品を検索できるか

16. 話し手は次の会議で何をすると言っていますか。

(A) 売上報告を発表する
(B) 新しい従業員を紹介する
(C) 昇進を知らせる
(D) アンケート結果を共有する

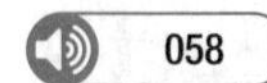

Questions 17 through 19 refer to the following instructions.

M Hi, everyone. I'm Min-Soo, brand manager here at Peridot Toys. I coordinate focus groups for the company. Thanks for coming in to give us your opinions on our new line of toy cars. For the prototype we're showing you today, we'd like to draw your attention to the packaging, in particular. We'll be asking you to assess the package on factors like visual appeal and how easy or difficult it is to open. Many companies make similar toys, and we want to ensure that our product stands out in the market. Please share your impressions. And before we begin, the nondisclosure forms are right here.

問題 17-19 は次の説明に関するものです。

皆さん、こんにちは。私は Min-Soo と申しまして、当 Peridot 玩具社のブランドマネージャーです。当社でフォーカスグループの調整役をしております。当社のおもちゃの自動車の新商品ラインにご意見を頂戴するためにお越しくださり、ありがとうございます。本日お見せする試作品に関しては、特にパッケージにご注目いただきたいと思います。見た目の魅力や、開封しやすいか、しにくいかといった要素について、パッケージを評価してくださいますようお願いいたします。多くの会社がよく似たおもちゃを作っていますので、当社の商品が市場で人目を引くよう万全を期したいと考えています。皆さんの印象をお聞かせください。では、始める前に、こちらが秘密保持契約書です。

17. 聞き手たちは何に参加していると思われますか。

(A) 株主総会
(B) フォーカスグループ
(C) 契約交渉
(D) 経営ワークショップ

18. 話し手によると、聞き手たちは何に注目するべきですか。

(A) 販売数量
(B) 最終期限
(C) 写真
(D) パッケージ

19. 話し手は "the nondisclosure forms are right here" という発言で、何を示唆していますか。

(A) 彼は早めに退席する必要がある。
(B) 彼は課題を終えた。
(C) 聞き手たちはある書類に記入しなければならない。
(D) 聞き手たちはすでに雇用されている。

Section 10 正解／スクリプト／訳

正解一覧

Part 1	**1** (B)					
Part 2	**2** (A)	**3** (A)	**4** (A)	**5** (B)	**6** (B)	**7** (A)
Part 3	**8** (B)	**9** (B)	**10** (C)	**11** (C)	**12** (D)	**13** (C)
Part 4	**14** (D)	**15** (C)	**16** (B)	**17** (A)	**18** (C)	**19** (B)

Part 1

1. Look at the picture marked number 1 in your test book.
問題用紙の 1 の写真を見てください。

W

(A) A worker is folding an apron. — 従業員がエプロンをたたんでいる。
(B) A worker is looking into a storage bin. — 従業員が保存容器をのぞき込んでいる。
(C) A worker is bending over a sink. — 従業員がシンクの上に身を屈めている。
(D) A worker is cleaning a microwave oven. — 従業員が電子レンジを掃除している。

Part 2

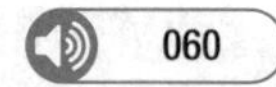

2. M How many people will be touring the building site? 何人の人々が建築現場を視察するのですか。

W (A) There'll be at least twelve. 少なくとも 12 人にはなるでしょう。
(B) Because the Web site's under construction. ウェブサイトが準備中だからです。
(C) No, it begins at ten A.M. いいえ、それは午前 10 時に始まります。

3. M Where is flight 42 departing from? 42 便はどこから出発しますか。

W (A) Sorry, it's been canceled. 申し訳ありません、その便は運休になりました。
(B) It's about a seven-hour flight. 約 7 時間のフライトです。
(C) A window seat, please. 窓側の座席をお願いします。

4. W You're serving that delicious cake at the event, right? あのおいしいケーキをイベントで出すのですね?

M (A) It's everyone's favorite. 皆のお気に入りですので。
(B) The birthday party was noisy. 誕生日パーティーは騒がしかったです。
(C) Ten dollars, please. 10 ドル、お願いします。

5. W Don't you want to go to the play? その芝居を見に行きたくはないのですか。

M (A) They played a good game. 彼らはいい試合をしました。
(B) Yes, but I have a lot of work to do. 行きたいのですが、やるべき仕事がたくさんあるのです。
(C) They live on Seventh Avenue. 彼らは 7 番街に住んでいます。

6. M Who repaired this window? 誰がこの窓を修理したのですか。

W (A) It's windy outside. 外は風が強いです。
(B) I was on vacation at the time. 私はそのとき休暇中だったのです。
(C) No, each department. いいえ、各部署です。

7. W We should order pens with our logo to give to customers. 顧客に配る当社ロゴ入りのペンを発注した方がいいと思います。

M (A) OK, good idea. 分かりました、良い案ですね。
(B) Turn left at the corner. その角を左に曲がってください。
(C) When did he go? 彼はいつ行ったのですか。

Part 3

061

Questions 8 through 10 refer to the following conversation with three speakers.

問題 8-10 は 3 人の話し手による次の会話に関するものです。

M1 We only have a week to complete the electrical work in this new wing of the hospital. Maria, you and I will take care of the lights in the patient rooms, and Sameer, you'll be working in the hallway.

この新しい病棟の電気工事を終えるのに 1 週間しかありません。Maria、あなたと私が病室の照明を担当しましょう、それから Sameer、あなたは廊下の作業をやってください。

M2 Wow, a week isn't a lot of time to install a new lighting system.

うわあ、新しい照明システムを設置するのに 1 週間では少ないですよ。

M1 True, but next week the painters will be coming to paint the walls, so we have to finish before that.

確かにそうですが、来週は塗装工が来て壁を塗るので、私たちはその前に終わらせなければなりません。

W Well, we'd better get started, then. I'll go to the truck and start unloading our supplies and equipment.

なるほど、それでは、取り掛かった方がいいですね。私はトラックまで行って備品や機材を降ろし始めます。

8. 話し手たちは誰だと思われますか。

(A) 医師
(B) 電気技師
(C) 建築士
(D) 検査技師

9. 来週何が行われる予定ですか。

(A) 建物の案内ツアーが実施される。
(B) 壁が塗装される。
(C) 新しい家具が配達される。
(D) 招待講演者が発表を行う。

10. 女性は次に何をすると言っていますか。

(A) 標識を掲示する
(B) 予定表を更新する
(C) 車から資材を降ろす
(D) 研究室のドアの鍵を開ける

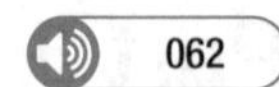

Questions 11 through 13 refer to the following conversation and badge.

問題 11-13 は次の会話と社員証に関するものです。

W Morning, David. I'm sure glad to see you! My badge won't open the door anymore. How do I get into the office building?

おはようございます、David。あなたに会えて本当によかったです！私の社員証では、もうどうにもドアが開かないんです。どうやってオフィスビルに入ればいいのでしょう？

M We can't scan our badges anymore; use the keypad by the door.

社員証のスキャンはもうできなくなっていて、ドアの横にあるキーパッドを使うんですよ。

W So, I just enter my ID number?

では、自分の ID 番号を入力するだけですか。

M No. The number under the bar code. Just the first four digits.

いいえ。バーコードの下にある番号です。最初の 4 桁だけです。

W Thanks. Since the company merger became official last week, there've been too many new processes to keep track of.

ありがとう。先週、会社の合併が正式なものになって以来、新しい手順が多過ぎて追いきれないんですよ。

M Yeah, when I was here on Saturday to bring in some paintings to decorate my office, the security guard had to tell me how to get inside.

ええ、私がオフィスに飾る絵を持って土曜日にここに来たときには、警備員に中に入る方法を教えてもらわなければなりませんでしたよ。

Irina Lachapelle
社員 ID：1796-021
部署コード：4328

バーコード：

11. 図を見てください。女性はどの番号を入力しますか。

(A) 1796
(B) 4328
(C) 5012
(D) 3452

12. 先週、何がありましたか。

(A) 社員証が 1 枚紛失した。
(B) 取引先との昼食会が開催された。
(C) 安全点検が行われた。
(D) 会社の合併が成立した。

13. なぜ男性は土曜日にビルに入館しようとしましたか。

(A) 眼鏡を取ってくるため
(B) イベントでボランティアをするため
(C) 美術品を持ち込むため
(D) 研修会の準備をするため

Part 4

063

Questions 14 through 16 refer to the following telephone message.

W Hello, I'm calling to update you on the design of your shop's Web site. I received the file with the photos you want to display on your home page. I'm sure there's a way I can make them load quickly. Now, I have a question for you regarding your domain name. I know you wanted to use the full name of your shop in the Web address, but that domain name is already taken. There's a shortened version that hasn't been purchased yet, though. I'd like to get your opinion about it. Keep in mind, availability can change quickly.

問題 14-16 は次の電話のメッセージに関するものです。

もしもし、貴店のウェブサイトのデザインについて最新情報をお伝えするためにお電話しています。ホームページへの掲載をお望みの写真ファイルを受け取りました。こうしたものを素早く読み込ませる方法は確かにございます。さて、ドメイン名についてお尋ねしたいことがあります。ウェブサイトのアドレスに貴店名をフルネームで使用することをご希望だったと存じますが、そのドメイン名はすでに使われています。ですが、まだ購入されていない短縮版のドメイン名が1つあります。この件について、ご意見をお聞かせください。ご留意いただきたいのですが、購入可能かどうかの状況はすぐに変わる可能性があります。

14. 話し手はどんな分野で働いていると思われますか。

(A) 接客
(B) 金融
(C) 不動産
(D) ウェブサイトのデザイン

15. 話し手は何を受け取ったと言っていますか。

(A) 物件のパンフレット
(B) 最新の請求書
(C) 写真
(D) 取引先からの意見

16. 話し手はなぜ "availability can change quickly" と言っていますか。

(A) 採用計画の正当性を示すため
(B) 速やかな回答を促すため
(C) 推薦に異議を唱えるため
(D) キャンセルについて謝罪するため

Section 10

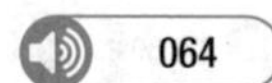

Questions 17 through 19 refer to the following talk.

M Thanks for coming out to Maple Wood Farm to hear about the employment opportunities we have coming up. Please be sure to pick up an information packet from the table by the entrance. We're a pretty big farm — we have 95,000 sugar maple trees on 5,000 acres of land. But I need to make sure that everyone understands the nature of the work. Some of you might be looking for something year-round, but our production season is from February to April. So keep that in mind. Now, I'd like to start by taking you outside and showing you how we hammer the taps into sugar maple trees.

問題 17-19 は次の話に関するものです。

当園がこの度設ける雇用機会について話を聞くためにMaple Wood農場へお越しいただき、ありがとうございます。入り口のそばにあるテーブルから資料一式をお忘れなくお取りください。当園はかなり広い農場です―― 5,000エーカーの土地に9万5,000本のサトウカエデの木があります。ですが、ぜひとも皆さんにこの仕事の性質を理解していただく必要がございます。皆さんの中には通年の仕事をお探しの方もいらっしゃるかもしれませんが、当園の生産シーズンは2月から4月です。ですから、その点にご留意ください。さて、まずは皆さんを外にお連れして、サトウカエデの木に採取口を打ち込む方法をお見せすることから始めたいと思います。

17. 話し手は聞き手たちに入り口で何をするよう頼んでいますか。

(A) 資料を取る
(B) 防護服を着る
(C) 受付票に名前を書く
(D) 就職申込書を預ける

18. 話し手は "our production season is from February to April" という発言で、何を意味していますか。

(A) 彼はもうそれ以上の注文をしない。
(B) 彼は4月まで対応できない。
(C) 彼は期間限定の仕事を提供している。
(D) 彼は生産シーズンを延ばしたいと思っている。

19. 聞き手たちは次に何をすると思われますか。

(A) サンプルを味見する
(B) 実演を見る
(C) 配達トラックから荷物を降ろす
(D) 木を植える

Section 11 正解／スクリプト／訳

正解一覧

Part 1	**1** (D)					
Part 2	**2** (A)	**3** (A)	**4** (B)	**5** (A)	**6** (B)	**7** (B)
Part 3	**8** (B)	**9** (C)	**10** (A)	**11** (B)	**12** (B)	**13** (D)
Part 4	**14** (B)	**15** (A)	**16** (C)	**17** (B)	**18** (C)	**19** (A)

Part 1

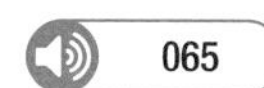

1. Look at the picture marked number 1 in your test book.
問題用紙の 1 の写真を見てください。

M
(A) Some handouts are being distributed.
資料が配布されているところである。

(B) They're seated in a circle.
彼らは輪になって座っている。

(C) One of the women is typing on a keyboard.
女性の 1 人はキーボードを打っている。

(D) The man is wearing a tie.
男性はネクタイをしている。

Part 2

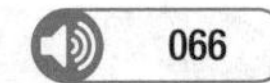

2. W Don't you think this room needs better lighting?
この部屋には、もっと良い照明が必要だと思いませんか。

M (A) Yes, I'll see if I can find a nice lamp.
そうですね、すてきなランプが見つかるかどうか調べてみます。

(B) He's getting better and better.
彼はどんどんうまくなっています。

(C) Are you sure it's not too tight?
本当にきつ過ぎませんか?

3. M You double-checked both sales reports, right?
どちらの売上報告書もダブルチェックしたのですよね?

W (A) Natasha did it yesterday.
昨日、Natashaがしました。

(B) We only accept cash.
当店は現金のみを受け付けております。

(C) Yes, turn right here.
はい、ここで右に曲がってください。

4. M Would you like to order dessert?
デザートのご注文はいかがですか。

W (A) The files are in order.
ファイルは整頓されています。

(B) I don't see chocolate cake on the menu.
メニューにチョコレートケーキが見当たりませんね。

(C) A table by the window.
窓際のテーブルです。

5. M Don't you have any software engineers on staff?
職員にソフトウエアエンジニアはいないのですか。

W (A) Yes, we rely on their expertise.
いますよ、私たちは彼らの専門知識を頼りにしています。

(B) I hope you had a good time.
お楽しみいただけたことと思います。

(C) That's not too far.
そこはあまり遠くありません。

6. W Would you prefer to meet in your office or mine?
あなたの執務室と私の執務室のどちらで打ち合わせするのがいいですか。

M (A) Her office assistant.
彼女の事務アシスタントです。

(B) I don't have any extra chairs.
私の所には余分な椅子がありません。

(C) Thanks, I bought it last week.
ありがとう、先週それを購入しました。

7. M Weren't you going on a business trip this week?
今週、出張に行くのではなかったのですか。

W (A) This house is vacant.
この家は空き家です。

(B) My client rescheduled our meeting.
取引先が打ち合わせの予定を変更したのです。

(C) She works for a travel magazine.
彼女は旅行雑誌の仕事をしています。

Part 3

067

Questions 8 through 10 refer to the following conversation.

問題 8-10 は次の会話に関するものです。

M Hello, you've reached In-Step Dance Costumes. How may I help you?

はい、In-Step ダンス衣装社でございます。どのようなご用件でしょうか。

W Hi. I'm interested in buying 50 top hats for a school performance. Do you have them in stock?

こんにちは。学校公演用にシルクハットを 50 個購入したいと思っています。在庫はありますか。

M Let me check our inventory. Oh — we do! If you'd like, I can set the hats aside and you can pick them up at our store here in Radcliffe.

在庫リストを確認させてください。ああ――ございますよ！もしよろしければ私が帽子を確保しておき、Radcliffe の当店店舗でお客さまにお受け取りいただくこともできますが。

W Radcliffe is two hours away.

Radcliffe まで 2 時間かかるんです。

M OK. In that case, I can ship them to you with a delivery date of next Friday. I just need your contact information to process the order. What's your address?

分かりました。それでしたら、来週金曜日のお届けにて商品を発送できます。ご注文手続きにはお客さまのご連絡先が必要です。ご住所はどちらですか。

8. 女性はどんな種類の商品について電話をかけていますか。

(A) 靴
(B) 帽子
(C) 上着
(D) スカート

9. 女性は "Radcliffe is two hours away" という発言で、何を示唆していますか。

(A) 同僚の手助けが必要である。
(B) Radcliffe でイベントを開催したい。
(C) Radcliffe まで行きたくない。
(D) 期限を延ばすことはできない。

10. 男性は次に何をしますか。

(A) 注文を処理する
(B) ウェブサイトへのリンクを E メールで送る
(C) 誤りを正す
(D) 店長と話す

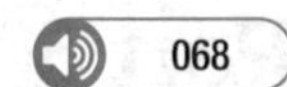

Questions 11 through 13 refer to the following conversation and printing information.

問題 11-13 は次の会話と印刷情報に関するものです。

M Welcome to Taylor Print Shop.

W Hi, I need a thousand copies of this concert program.

M Sure. We can have that ready for you tomorrow evening.

W Oh, can't you do it now? The concert is tomorrow afternoon.

M Normally we could, but all our staff are working on a rush job. You could use our self-service machines.

W Well, I want them in color, and stapled.

M We have an advanced color copier right here that you can use. Just pay at the counter when you're done.

Taylor 印刷店へようこそ。

こんにちは、このコンサートプログラムが 1,000 部必要なんです。

かしこまりました。明日の夕方にはご用意できますよ。

えっ、今すぐやってもらえませんか。コンサートは明日の午後なんです。

普段ならできるのですが、スタッフ全員で急ぎの仕事にかかりきりなのです。よろしければセルフサービス機をお使いいただけますよ。

えっと、プログラムはカラーで、ホチキス留めしたいのですが。

すぐこちらにご利用になれる高機能カラーコピー機がございます。お済みになったらカウンターでお支払いください。

Taylor 印刷店	
コピー機種	
M-20	標準 — モノクロ
M-30	高機能 — モノクロ
M-50	標準 — カラー
M-60	高機能 — カラー

11. 女性は何のコピーを必要としていますか。

(A) 写真
(B) コンサートプログラム
(C) 財務報告書
(D) パーティーの招待状

12. 男性はスタッフについて何と言っていますか。

(A) 講習会に出ている。
(B) 仕事で手が離せない。
(C) 最近雇われた。
(D) 勤務時間がそろそろ終わる。

13. 図を見てください。女性はどのコピー機種を使うと思われますか。

(A) M-20
(B) M-30
(C) M-50
(D) M-60

Part 4

069

Questions 14 through 16 refer to the following telephone message.

問題 14-16 は次の電話のメッセージに関するものです。

M Hello, Aisha. This is Paul, calling from the art gallery. I wanted to give you some information about next week's art show. We'll need your painting to be at the gallery no later than three P.M. on Wednesday. And I know you asked if you should bring hooks and wire to hang it up, but don't worry, we'll handle the setup ourselves. Naturally, we understand artists are concerned about the safety of their pieces, but our workers are very experienced. Anyway, we're very happy to be able to display your work in our gallery. See you soon!

もしもし、Aisha。Paul です、美術館からお電話差し上げています。来週の美術展の情報をお伝えしたかったのです。あなたの絵画は、水曜日の午後 3 時までに美術館に届いている必要があります。それと、絵をつるすフックやワイヤーを持参した方がいいかというお問い合わせを頂いていましたが、心配はご無用です。設置は当館で行います。もちろん、アーティストの皆さんがご自身の作品の安全を気にされることは理解していますが、当館の作業員は非常に経験豊かです。いずれにせよ、当美術館にあなたの作品を展示できることをとてもうれしく思っています。それではまた！

14. 聞き手は誰だと思われますか。

(A) 建設作業員
(B) アーティスト
(C) ヘアスタイリスト
(D) 教師

15. 話し手によると、聞き手は何について尋ねましたか。

(A) 資材を持参するかどうか
(B) どこで仕事仲間に会えばいいか
(C) どのように支払いをすればいいか
(D) いつ申込書を提出すればいいか

16. 話し手は "our workers are very experienced" という発言で、何を意味していますか。

(A) 作業員は昇給を受けるべきである。
(B) 作業員は特別な資格を取得している。
(C) 作業員は品物を傷つけない。
(D) 作業員は現在手が空いていない。

070

Questions 17 through 19 refer to the following introduction.

M Welcome, everyone, to this last event in the bookstore's spring speaker series. We're pleased to be ending with a local writer, the novelist Elise Weber. Ms. Weber will be reading from her latest book, *In the Park*. The novel's set in the Stanton neighborhood, known to have the oldest homes in the city, and the story takes place nearly two hundred years ago. Before Ms. Weber begins, let me apologize. We don't have copies available for everyone who wants to purchase the novel. We have a very large crowd today. We've ordered more books, which should be available for sale later in the week.

問題 17-19 は次の紹介に関するものです。

皆さん、当書店の春の講演会シリーズのこの最終イベントへようこそ。地元の作家である小説家の Elise Weber さんをお迎えして会を締めくくれることをうれしく思います。Weber さんには、ご自身の最新作『公園にて』から朗読していただきます。この小説は、市内でも最も古い家々があることで知られている Stanton 地区に舞台が設定されており、物語は 200 年近く前から始まります。Weber さんに始めていただく前に、おわびをさせてください。当店にはこの小説のご購入を希望される皆さん全員に行き渡るほどの部数がございません。本日は大勢のお客さまにお越しいただいています。当店では追加の本を注文済みで、それらは今週の後半にはご購入いただけるはずです。

17. Elise Weber とは誰ですか。

(A) 建築家
(B) 作家
(C) 映画製作者
(D) 写真家

18. Stanton 地区は何で知られていますか。

(A) 美しい景観
(B) 多種多様な住民
(C) 長い歴史
(D) 美術館

19. 話し手はなぜ "We have a very large crowd today" と言っていますか。

(A) 問題の理由を説明するため
(B) 広告キャンペーンへの満足を表すため
(C) 別の店舗を見つけることを提案するため
(D) 同僚の決定を疑問視するため

Section 12 正解／スクリプト／訳

正解一覧

Part 1	**1** (C)					
Part 2	**2** (B)	**3** (C)	**4** (B)	**5** (C)	**6** (B)	**7** (B)
Part 3	**8** (B)	**9** (A)	**10** (C)	**11** (D)	**12** (A)	**13** (C)
Part 4	**14** (A)	**15** (B)	**16** (A)	**17** (C)	**18** (D)	**19** (B)

Part 1

1. Look at the picture marked number 1 in your test book.
問題用紙の 1 の写真を見てください。

M
(A) Some maintenance workers are washing a van.
数人の保守作業員がワゴン車を洗っている。

(B) Some customers are handing money to a cashier.
数人の客がレジ係にお金を渡している。

(C) Some people are walking under an awning.
数人の人々が日よけの下を歩いている。

(D) Some boxes are being stacked in a corner.
幾つかの箱が隅に積まれているところである。

Part 2

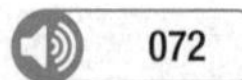

2. M Where can I find an extra clipboard? 予備のクリップボードはどこにありますか。

W (A) The black pen, please. 黒のペンをお願いします。
(B) You can use mine. 私のを使っていいですよ。
(C) We're out of paper clips. ペーパークリップを切らしています。

3. W Excuse me, when will our food be ready? すみません、私たちの料理はいつできますか。

M (A) A trip to the orchard. 果樹園訪問です。
(B) I saw him recently. 最近、彼を見かけました。
(C) The kitchen is very busy tonight. 今夜は厨房が大変混み合っておりまして。

4. M I'd love to have Mohammed speak at the reception. 歓迎会ではぜひ Mohammed にスピーチをしてもらいたいのですが。

W (A) No, I have a receipt. いいえ、レシートを持っています。
(B) You should ask him! 彼に聞いてみるべきです！
(C) The tea is a bit weak. この紅茶は少し薄いです。

5. M We should replace the coffee machine in the break room. 休憩室のコーヒーマシンを交換した方がいいと思います。

W (A) Is this seat taken? この席はふさがっていますか。
(B) Yes, just a glass of milk. はい、牛乳を1杯だけ。
(C) We bought this one in January. これは1月に買ったんですよ。

6. W Who's going to manage the new branch location? 誰が新しい支社を経営するのでしょうか。

M (A) Yes, let's trim that tree. はい、その木を刈りましょう。
(B) I know someone who's applying for the position. 私はその職に応募している人を知っていますよ。
(C) Can you pick me up at the park? 公園まで車で迎えに来てもらえますか。

7. M I heard your new book was just published! あなたの新しい本がちょうど出版されたところだと聞きましたよ！

W (A) Please stand closer to one another. 互いにもっと近づいて立ってください。
(B) I have some extra copies. 何冊か余分を持っていますよ。
(C) A magazine stand. 雑誌売店です。

Part 3

Questions 8 through 10 refer to the following conversation with three speakers.

問題8-10は3人の話し手による次の会話に関するものです。

M1 I assume you've had a chance to read the company's annual report. It does a good job of highlighting last year's accomplishments, like reduced operating expenses, and also includes next year's objectives. Any questions?

あなた方は会社の年次報告書に目を通す機会があったことと思います。営業経費の削減といった昨年の成果を分かりやすく強調していますし、来年の目標も記載されています。何かご質問は?

M2 According to the report, next year's big initiative is to procure next generation high-speed trains for the rail network. Is there a time frame for this initiative?

報告書によると、来年の大きな構想は鉄道網に次世代型高速列車を調達することですね。この構想の時間枠は決まっていますか。

M1 Well, as you can see on page 30 of the report, it mostly depends on the availability of government funding. It's not yet clear how much money we'll receive next year.

ええと、報告書の30ページにあるように、それは主として政府からの財政援助を得られるかどうか次第です。来年どのくらいの資金を得られるかは、まだはっきりしていません。

W Actually, a government representative is visiting our office tomorrow. He'll update us on the status of our funding request.

実は明日、政府の当局者が当事務所を訪れることになっています。彼は財政援助要請の状況についての最新情報を私たちに話してくれるでしょう。

8. 会話の目的は何ですか。

(A) 決済処理を見直すこと
(B) 年次報告書について話し合うこと
(C) 慈善行事を企画すること
(D) 売買契約を取り決めること

9. 会社は何を購入したいのですか。

(A) 列車
(B) 倉庫
(C) コンピューター
(D) 船

10. 話し手たちは明日、何をする予定ですか。

(A) 製品を検査する
(B) 従業員の研修を行う
(C) 政府の役人と会う
(D) 助成金の申請書を提出する

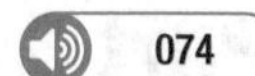

Questions 11 through 13 refer to the following conversation and museum map.

W Welcome to the Fairwood Museum of Modern Art. How can I help you?

M Hello, I'm doing research for a book I'm writing about the painter Dominique Lachapelle. I understand you have some of her oil paintings here.

W We do. Normally Lachapelle's works are on display, but the oil painting gallery is currently closed for renovations.

M I see. When will it reopen? I'm hoping to finish that section of my book soon.

W It will be closed all month. I suggest you speak with the director of the museum. We put Lachapelle's paintings in storage, but you may be able to schedule a private viewing.

問題 11-13 は次の会話と美術館の館内図に関するものです。

Fairwood 近代美術館へようこそ。どのようなご用件でしょうか。

こんにちは。私は今執筆している、画家 Dominique Lachapelle に関する本のために調べ物をしています。こちらに彼女の油絵が何点かありますよね。

ございます。通常でしたら Lachapelle の作品は展示されているのですが、油絵の展示室は現在改装のため閉鎖中なのです。

なるほど。いつ再開される予定ですか。私は本のそのセクションを近日中に書き終えたいと思っているのですが。

今月いっぱい閉鎖の予定です。美術館の館長と話されてはいかがでしょう。Lachapelle の絵は倉庫に保管していますが、内覧のご予定を組めるかもしれません。

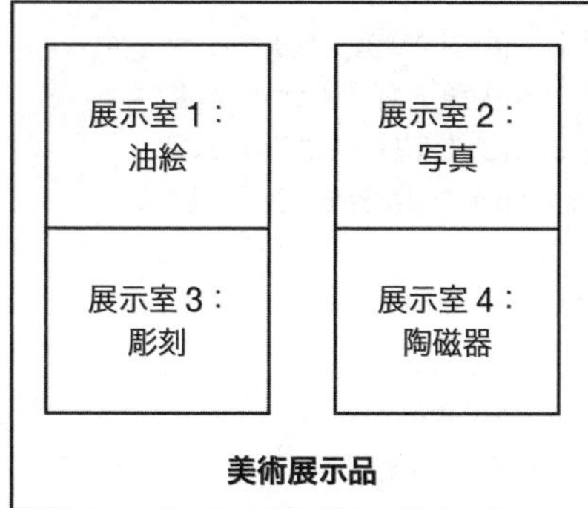

11. なぜ男性は美術館を訪れていますか。

(A) ツアーに参加するため
(B) 寄付をするため
(C) 贈り物を購入するため
(D) 本のために調べ物をするため

12. 図を見てください。女性はどの展示室が現在閉鎖中だと言っていますか。

(A) 展示室 1
(B) 展示室 2
(C) 展示室 3
(D) 展示室 4

13. 女性は何をすることを提案していますか。

(A) 美術の個人指導を受けること
(B) 客員講座に参加すること
(C) 美術館の館長と話すこと
(D) オンラインで展示品を見ること

Part 4

075

Questions 14 through 16 refer to the following speech.

問題 14-16 は次のスピーチに関するものです。

M Thank you all for coming tonight. We're celebrating the tenth anniversary of Collings Incorporated! I began this company with a small office in Seattle, and now, just a decade later, we have offices in major cities across the country. This is truly thanks to all your hard work. I'm also pleased to announce that our first overseas office will open just after the New Year! OK, I have some exciting prizes to give out. The names of everyone attending are in this bowl here. If I pick your name, you'll get to choose a prize from this table.

今夜はご来場ありがとうございます。これは Collings 社 10 周年記念の祝賀会です！私はシアトルの小さな事務所からこの会社を始めました。そして、わずか 10 年後の今、当社は全国の主要都市に事務所を構えています。これはまさに皆さんの懸命な働きのおかげです。また、当社初の海外事務所が年明け早々にオープンするとお伝えできることをうれしく思います！さて、わくわくするような賞品の数々をお配りしたいと思います。ご出席の皆さん全員のお名前が、ここにあるこの器に入っています。私がお名前を引き当てた方には、このテーブルから賞品を 1 つ選んでいただきます。

14. どんな出来事が祝われていますか。

(A) 会社の記念日
(B) 製品発売
(C) 国民の祝日
(D) 定年退職

15. 話し手によると、会社は年明けに何をしますか。

(A) 新たな役員を選出する
(B) 海外に事務所を開く
(C) 他社と合併する
(D) 広告キャンペーンを開始する

16. 次に何が行われますか。

(A) 賞品が渡される。
(B) 食べ物が提供される。
(C) 動画が映される。
(D) バンドが演奏を始める。

076

Questions 17 through 19 refer to the following telephone message.

W Hi, Vladimir. This is Li Wang from Smith Attorneys. I have some information about the condominiums your company wants to develop in Spring City. Our legal team completed a preliminary review of your proposal. We discovered a possible problem — the land is partially zoned for commercial use. This could be a significant issue since you want to build residences on the site. But, you know, many residential buildings have retail space on the ground floor. We'll need to discuss this issue before formally submitting your proposal to the city's zoning committee. Their next meeting is in two weeks, so we'll need to talk soon.

問題 17-19 は次の電話のメッセージに関するものです。

もしもし、Vladimir ですか。Smith 法律事務所の Li Wang です。御社が Spring 市で開発を希望されている分譲マンションに関してお知らせがあります。当事務所の法務チームが御社の計画書の予備審査を完了しました。問題になり得る点が 1 つ見つかりました——土地の一部が商業用途に指定されています。御社は現地に集合住宅を建てたいわけですから、これは重大な問題になりかねません。とはいえ、ご承知の通り、多くの居住用ビルは 1 階に店舗スペースがあります。市の地域区分指定委員会に正式に計画書を提出する前に、私たちはこの問題について議論する必要があるでしょう。次の委員会は 2 週間後なので、私たちは早々に話し合わなければなりません。

17. 話し手はどんな種類の会社で働いていますか。

(A) 広告代理店
(B) デパート
(C) 法律事務所
(D) 銀行

18. 話し手はなぜ "many residential buildings have retail space on the ground floor" と言っていますか。

(A) 決定について説明するため
(B) 同意を表すため
(C) 誤りを正すため
(D) 提案をするため

19. 話し手によると、2 週間後に何がありますか。

(A) 支払期限が来る。
(B) 委員会が開かれる。
(C) 見学ツアーが行われる。
(D) 製品が発売される。

Section 13 正解／スクリプト／訳

正解一覧

Part 1	**1** (D)					
Part 2	**2** (B)	**3** (A)	**4** (C)	**5** (B)	**6** (A)	**7** (C)
Part 3	**8** (A)	**9** (B)	**10** (D)	**11** (B)	**12** (A)	**13** (C)
Part 4	**14** (A)	**15** (B)	**16** (C)	**17** (A)	**18** (C)	**19** (B)

Part 1

1. Look at the picture marked number 1 in your test book.
問題用紙の 1 の写真を見てください。

W
(A) Some people have dropped bags on a step.
数人が踏み段にバッグを落とした。
(B) Some people are walking up the stairs.
数人が階段を上がっている。
(C) One person is putting on a hat.
1 人が帽子をかぶろうとしている。
(D) One person is holding a handrail.
1 人が手すりを握っている。

Part 2

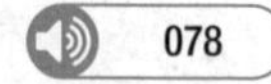
078

2. M Who did the board decide to hire? 取締役会は誰を採用することにしたのですか。

W (A) Sales should start tomorrow. 販売は明日開始になるはずです。
(B) They listened to our recommendation! 彼らは私たちの推薦を聞き入れてくれました！
(C) That's the best option on the menu. それはメニューの中で一番良い選択ですね。

3. W Will you be free around three P.M. to meet with our Malaysian marketing team? 午後３時頃、マレーシアのマーケティングチームと打ち合わせをする時間はありますか。

M (A) No, I've got a conference call then. いいえ、その時間は電話会議があるのです。
(B) There's a supermarket nearby. 近くにスーパーがあります。
(C) It's so nice to meet you! お会いできてとてもうれしいです！

4. W The office renovations will be noisy. 事務所の改装で騒がしくなるでしょう。

W (A) No, by invitation only. いいえ、招待された人のみです。
(B) It's on the desk by the window. 窓際の机の上にあります。
(C) I'll be working from home. 私は在宅勤務するつもりです。

5. M I'd like you to come in to work at seven A.M. tomorrow. 明日は午前７時に出勤してもらいたいのですが。

W (A) A free breakfast. 無料の朝食です。
(B) The bus service doesn't start until nine. バスの運行が９時にならないと始まらないのです。
(C) Yes, I liked them. はい、私はそれらが気に入りました。

6. W What is the presentation going to be about? プレゼンテーションは何に関するものになるのですか。

M (A) I'm not really sure. 私はあまりよく知りません。
(B) No, he already bought a present. いいえ、彼はもうプレゼントを買いました。
(C) At the airport. 空港で。

7. M Can't we replace the motor instead of buying a new sewing machine? 新しいミシンを買う代わりに、モーターを交換できませんか。

W (A) This is a nice place. ここは素敵な場所です。
(B) One of our best workers. うちの最も優秀な働き手の一人です。
(C) That machine is very old. あのミシンはすごく古いですから。

Part 3

Questions 8 through 10 refer to the following conversation.

問題 8-10 は次の会話に関するものです。

M Thanks for picking me up, Amal. Wow, I like your new car — you even have seat warmers! I bet that makes driving in cold weather more comfortable.

迎えに来てくれてありがとう、Amal。わあ、すてきな新車ですね——座席ヒーターまで付いているなんて！ これがあればきっと、寒い時期の運転もより快適でしょうね。

W I've only had this car for a month.

この車を手に入れてまだ 1 カ月なんですよ。

M Ah, I see. Well, then you have something to look forward to this winter. So, do you know how to get to the conference center?

ああ、なるほど。ええと、それなら、この冬に楽しみなことができましたね。それで、協議会場への行き方は分かりますか。

W Yep — I've driven there before. Say — do you mind if we talk about our conference presentation while I drive?

ええ——あそこへは前に車で行ったことがあります。そうだ——運転しながら、協議会での発表について話しても構いませんか。

M Sure. So, I'll start by giving an overview of the most common medicines prescribed to treat headaches. After that, you'll introduce our research study on alleviating headaches through exercise. Then, I'll conclude by explaining our findings.

もちろんです。では、まず私が頭痛を治療するのに処方される最も一般的な薬の概要から話を始めます。その後、あなたが運動を通じた頭痛緩和に関する私たちの調査研究を紹介します。それから、私が研究結果を説明して締めくくります。

8. 女性は "I've only had this car for a month" という発言で、何を示唆していますか。

(A) 自分の車の機能の 1 つを使ったことがない。
(B) 長距離の運転はしたくない。
(C) 修理が必要だと知って驚いている。
(D) 新車の購入に興味がない。

9. 話し手たちはどんなイベントに向かっていると思われますか。

(A) 祭り
(B) 協議会
(C) 講習会
(D) 製品発売イベント

10. 話し手たちはどんな業界で働いていると思われますか。

(A) 接客
(B) 運輸
(C) 報道機関
(D) 医療・保健

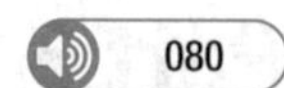

Questions 11 through 13 refer to the following conversation and train cars.

問題11-13は次の会話と列車車両に関するものです。

W Hi, Makoto, I'm glad you're here. We're short-staffed today.

お疲れさま、Makoto。あなたがここにいてくれてよかったです。今日は人手が足りません。

M How can I help?

何をお手伝いすればいいですか。

W We have a long line of customers wanting to purchase refreshments. Normally there's a second person serving customers, but right now it's just me. Do you have time to help me here?

軽食を買いたいお客さまの長い列ができています。いつもは接客をする人がもう1人いるのですが、今は私だけです。ここで私を手伝ってくれる時間はありますか。

M Sure. I do need to check the tickets of passengers in first class, but that can wait a few minutes.

はい。私は一等車の乗客の切符を確認する必要があるのですが、それは少し待てますから。

W Thank you! I'll only need your help for a little while. Another crew member will be boarding at the next stop.

ありがとうございます！あなたの手助けが必要なのは少しの間だけです。次の停車駅でもう1人乗務員が乗ってくることになっていますから。

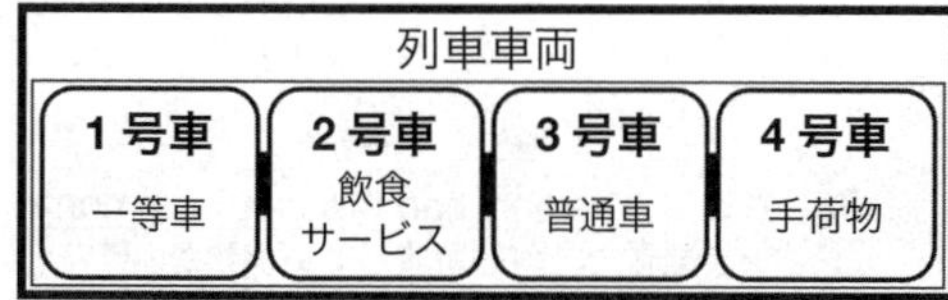

11. 図を見てください。話し手たちは現在どの車両にいますか。

(A) 1号車
(B) 2号車
(C) 3号車
(D) 4号車

12. 男性は何をする必要があると言っていますか。

(A) 切符を確認する
(B) 責任者に相談する
(C) アナウンスを行う
(D) 手荷物を収納する

13. 女性は次の停車駅で何が起こると言っていますか。

(A) 列車が線路を切り替える。
(B) 補給品が配達される。
(C) 同僚が列車に乗る。
(D) 保守作業が行われる。

Part 4

081

Questions 14 through 16 refer to the following announcement.

M Before we close the kitchen tonight, I have an announcement to make. On Thursday, a food writer will be coming in to sample some of our specialty dishes. A tourism magazine is writing an article about us, and we want to make a good impression. As part of this, we'll make dishes that we know are customer favorites. Also, I think this event would be a great time to perfect our serving techniques. So, I've printed out these instructions for serving special guests. Please review them carefully. I'll pass the copies around now.

問題 14-16 は次のお知らせに関するものです。

今夜は厨房を閉める前にお知らせがあります。木曜日に、フードライターが来店して、当店の名物料理を何品か試食します。観光雑誌が当店の記事を書いてくれることになっているので、良い印象を与えたいと思っています。この一環として、お客さま方のお気に入りであることが分かっている料理を作ります。また、今回の件は私たちの給仕技術に磨きをかける絶好の機会になると思います。そこで、特別なお客さまを給仕する際の指示をプリントアウトしました。しっかりおさらいしておいてください。今からコピーを回してお配りします。

14. このお知らせはどこで行われていると思われますか。

(A) レストラン
(B) スーパーマーケット
(C) 旅行代理店
(D) 出版社

15. 話し手によると、木曜日に何が起こりますか。

(A) 家電製品が修理される。
(B) ライターが訪れる。
(C) 商品が配達される。
(D) スタッフが研修を受ける。

16. 話し手は聞き手たちに何をするよう依頼していますか。

(A) 特別なユニフォームを受け取る
(B) 注文書を印刷する
(C) 指示をおさらいする
(D) 名前を覚える

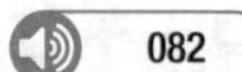

Questions 17 through 19 refer to the following talk.

W Thank you for inviting me to this seminar. It's a privilege to speak with this company's leadership on ways to save money on energy costs. For those who aren't familiar, my engineering firm specializes in finding ways for businesses to lower their electricity costs. One way to do this is to invest in renewable energies such as a solar energy system. Many companies are making these changes nowadays. You might have heard that solar energy systems are difficult to install, but actually that's not true. I'm going to show you a short video about how quickly these solar panels can be put onto your buildings.

問題 17-19 は次の話に関するものです。

このセミナーにお招きいただき、ありがとうございます。こちらの会社の幹部の方々とエネルギーコストの削減方法についてお話しできることを光栄に思います。ご存じない方のために申し上げますと、私のエンジニアリング会社は、企業様の電気代の削減方法を見つけることを専門としております。これを実現する1つの方法は、太陽光発電システムなどの再生可能エネルギーへの投資です。昨今、多くの企業様がこうした転換を行っています。太陽光発電システムは設置が難しいという話をお聞きになったことがあるかもしれませんが、実のところそれは事実ではありません。こうしたソーラーパネルをいかに速やかに御社の建物に設置できるかに関する短い動画をお見せしましょう。

17. 話し手は誰だと思われますか。

(A) 技術者
(B) 弁護士
(C) 銀行家
(D) 建築士

18. 話し手はなぜ "Many companies are making these changes nowadays" と言っていますか。

(A) 誤解を正すため
(B) 競争への懸念を表すため
(C) 購入を働きかけるため
(D) 遅れた理由を説明するため

19. 聞き手たちは次に何をしますか。

(A) 書式に記入する
(B) 動画を見る
(C) 安全装置を装着する
(D) 建物内を見学する

Section 14 正解／スクリプト／訳

正解一覧

Part 1	**1** (D)					
Part 2	**2** (B)	**3** (A)	**4** (A)	**5** (B)	**6** (A)	**7** (C)
Part 3	**8** (A)	**9** (B)	**10** (D)	**11** (B)	**12** (B)	**13** (C)
Part 4	**14** (D)	**15** (A)	**16** (A)	**17** (D)	**18** (C)	**19** (B)

Part 1

1. Look at the picture marked number 1 in your test book.

問題用紙の 1 の写真を見てください。

M

(A) She's stacking some boxes on the floor.
彼女は床に箱を積み重ねている。

(B) She's walking down a store aisle.
彼女は店の通路を歩いている。

(C) She's placing some products into a shopping cart.
彼女はショッピングカートに商品を入れている。

(D) She's reaching for some merchandise on a shelf.
彼女は棚の上の商品を取ろうと手を伸ばしている。

Part 2

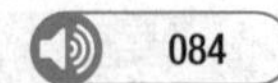

2\. W Why did we change the lunch menu? 当店はなぜランチメニューを変えたのですか。

M
(A) At the grocery store. 食料品店で。
(B) Weren't you at the staff meeting? スタッフ会議に出ていなかったのですか。
(C) No, I don't have any change. いいえ、小銭は持っていません。

3\. M Maybe we'll need to hire a recruiting firm to fill the managerial position. もしかすると、その管理職の空席を埋めるには人材紹介会社に依頼する必要があるかもしれません。

W
(A) We did get some good résumés today. 今日まさに幾つか良い履歴書が届きましたよ。
(B) No, put it on the lower shelf. いいえ、下の棚に入れてください。
(C) He should wear a suit and tie. 彼はスーツとネクタイを着用するべきです。

4\. W Is the train going to be delayed? この電車は遅れるのですか。

M
(A) Yes, that's what the information board says. はい、情報案内板にはそう書いてあります。
(B) Thanks for filling out the survey. 調査票のご記入、ありがとうございます。
(C) To a training session. 講習会へ。

5\. W Who's assigned to take the new employees on a tour? 誰が新入社員を案内する役目を割り当てられていますか。

W
(A) Just the main office building. 本社ビルだけです。
(B) That will be announced later today. 今日後ほど発表されます。
(C) There's room over there. あちらにスペースがあります。

6\. W Why isn't the library open today? なぜ今日は図書館が開いていないのですか。

M
(A) Because it's a holiday. 祝日だからです。
(B) Shut the window, please. 窓を閉めてください。
(C) No, the concert starts at twelve. いいえ、コンサートは12時に始まります。

7\. M Some soda has spilled in aisle seven. 7番通路に炭酸飲料がこぼれています。

W
(A) Unfortunately, that's our store policy. あいにくですが、それが当店の方針です。
(B) Wow, that's a good deal. わあ、それはお買い得ですね。
(C) OK, I'll go get a mop. 分かりました、モップを取ってきます。

Part 3

Questions 8 through 10 refer to the following conversation with three speakers.

問題8-10は3人の話し手による次の会話に関するものです。

W Hassan, this is George, our factory floor manager. He's going to start today's tour by showing you the full production line.

Hassan、こちらが現場責任者のGeorgeです。彼が全製造ラインのご案内から今日の見学ツアーを始めてくれることになっています。

M1 Hassan, welcome to Manefort Boats. After seeing our attention to quality, we hope you'll be interested in investing with us.

Hassan、Manefort小型船社へようこそ。弊社の品質へのこだわりをご覧いただいた後で、弊社への投資にご興味をお持ちいただけると幸いです。

M2 Nice to meet you, George. Well, so far I'm impressed with your line of boats, especially the X54 Cruiser — it's incredibly lightweight.

はじめまして、George。そうですね、これまでのところ御社の小型船の商品ラインに感銘を受けています。特にX54クルーザー——これは信じられないくらい軽量ですよね。

M1 Exactly, it's because we use a special composite of fiberglass and resins. It's a new process in the industry.

おっしゃる通りで、それはガラス繊維と樹脂の特殊な複合材を使用しているからなのです。業界でも新しい製法です。

M2 Oh? I'd like to learn more about that.

えっ？ そのことをもう少し詳しく知りたいですね。

W I'll go get you the design specification sheet for that model and then George can start the tour.

私がそのモデルの設計仕様書を取ってまいります。その後、Georgeに見学ツアーを始めてもらいましょう。

8. Hassanは誰だと思われますか。

(A) 投資家候補
(B) 訪問中の安全検査官
(C) 新しい従業員
(D) リピーターの顧客

9. 男性は、ある小型船について何が素晴らしいと言っていますか。

(A) 高速である。
(B) 軽量である。
(C) 低価格である。
(D) 燃費がよい。

10. 女性は何をすると言っていますか。

(A) 備品を注文する
(B) 登録フォームに記入する
(C) 支払いの予定を立てる
(D) 設計情報を提供する

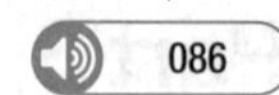

Questions 11 through 13 refer to the following conversation and poster.

W Hey, Akira. I finally tried that new noodle house today... the one two blocks from here.

M Oh, how was it?

W It was OK... it was kind of expensive. Anyway, at the restaurant, I saw a poster for a dance performance. I was thinking that some of us from work could go together.

M That sounds like fun, but I've been working the late shift from four P.M. till midnight. Are there any shows that I'd be able to attend?

W Don't worry. You can still go. See? I took a picture of the poster on my phone.

M Great! Can you send that to me?

問題11-13は次の会話とポスターに関するものです。

こんにちは、Akira。今日やっとあの新しい麺の店に行ってみましたよ…ここから2ブロック先のお店です。

おっ、どうでしたか。

まあまあでした…ちょっと高かったです。それはさておき、そのお店で、ダンス公演のポスターを見ました。職場の何人かで一緒に行けたらなあと思っていたのですが。

それは楽しそうだけど、私はこのところ午後4時から深夜までの遅番なんですよ。私も行けそうな公演はありますか。

ご心配なく。あなたもちゃんと行けますよ。ほらね。携帯にポスターの写真を撮ってきたんです。

素晴らしい！それ、私に送ってもらえますか。

11. 女性は飲食店について何と言っていますか。

(A) 騒がしかった。
(B) 高かった。
(C) 食事が味気なかった。
(D) 対応が遅かった。

12. 図を見てください。男性はいつ公演に行けると思われますか。

(A) 8月25日
(B) 8月26日
(C) 8月27日
(D) 8月28日

13. 男性は女性に何をするよう頼んでいますか。

(A) 友人に連絡する
(B) 予約を取る
(C) 写真を送る
(D) チケットを買う

Part 4

087

Questions 14 through 16 refer to the following broadcast.

M In local news, this week our very own Community Theater Company started rehearsals of its upcoming production of *Winslow Park* — and the company has just announced that the show will open next weekend. Preparations for a show of this size usually take months. You can purchase tickets at the door, but if you go online and buy them, you'll receive a ten percent discount! That's a good reason to plan ahead. Now, we have the show's star, Claudine Moreau, in the studio to tell us more about the production. Claudine, welcome!

問題 14-16 は次の放送に関するものです。

地元のニュースとして、今週、われらの地域劇団が次の上演作『ウィンスロー公園』のリハーサルを開始しました──劇団はつい先ほど、この公演が来週末開演予定であることを発表しました。この規模の公演準備は通常数カ月かかります。会場入り口でチケットを購入することもできますが、オンラインで購入すると 10 パーセント引きとなります！前もって計画すべき十分な理由になりますね。さて、公演で主役を務める Claudine Moreau をスタジオにお迎えしていますので、作品について詳しく語っていただきましょう。Claudine、ようこそ！

14. 話し手はなぜ "Preparations for a show of this size usually take months" と言っていますか。

(A) もっと多額の予算を要望するため
(B) 上演の遅れを説明するため
(C) プロジェクトのためのボランティアを探し出すため
(D) 成し遂げたことを強調するため

15. 聞き手たちはどうすれば割引を受けることができますか。

(A) オンラインで購入することによって
(B) アンケートに回答することによって
(C) オンラインでレビューを投稿することによって
(D) 団体チケットを購入することによって

16. 話し手は次に何をすると思われますか。

(A) ゲストにインタビューをする
(B) 賞を授与する
(C) 天気予報を伝える
(D) 聴取者からの電話に出る

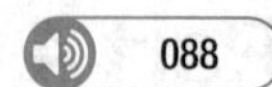

Questions 17 through 19 refer to the following instructions.

W I have some information for all front desk receptionists. Next month our office building is installing electronic lockers downstairs in the entryway. Here's how these lockers will work. A delivery service will have an access code for a specific locker, together with the name of a recipient. After leaving a package, the delivery person will notify that person by text or e-mail. In order to pick up the package, the recipient will scan a bar code, which will be included in the notification. Now, the best part of this new system is that receptionists will no longer have to sign for a delivery of a package. Are there any questions about this?

問題 17-19 は次の説明に関するものです。

受付係の皆さん全員にお知らせがあります。来月、当オフィスビルは1階の入り口通路に電子ロッカーを設置します。これらのロッカーの仕組みは次の通りです。宅配業者が所定のロッカーのアクセスコード、ならびに受取人の名前を用意します。配達員は荷物を収めた後、テキストメッセージまたはEメールで受取人に通知します。荷物を受け取るには、受取人はバーコードをスキャンしますが、そのバーコードは先ほどの通知の中に記載されています。さて、この新しいシステムの一番良いところは、受付の皆さんが荷物の受け取り時にサインをする必要がもはやなくなることです。以上についてご質問はありますか。

17. 聞き手たちは誰ですか。

(A) 工場の従業員
(B) 保守作業員
(C) 集合住宅の居住者
(D) 会社の受付係

18. 話し手は主に何について話していますか。

(A) どのようにフィードバックを伝えるか
(B) どのように施設が改修されるか
(C) どのように荷物が配達されるか
(D) どのように研修講座に登録するか

19. 新しいシステムのどんな利点が言及されていますか。

(A) 待ち時間が短くなる。
(B) サインが不要になる。
(C) 経費が削減される。
(D) 責任者が常時対応可能になる。

Section 15 正解／スクリプト／訳

正解一覧

Part 1	**1** (D)					
Part 2	**2** (C)	**3** (A)	**4** (B)	**5** (A)	**6** (B)	**7** (C)
Part 3	**8** (D)	**9** (D)	**10** (C)	**11** (B)	**12** (C)	**13** (B)
Part 4	**14** (B)	**15** (B)	**16** (A)	**17** (B)	**18** (D)	**19** (A)

Part 1

1. Look at the picture marked number 1 in your test book.

問題用紙の 1 の写真を見てください。

W (A) She's picking up a file folder.
(B) She's storing a broom in a closet.
(C) Mail is being sorted into slots.
(D) Clipboards have been hung in a row.

彼女は書類挟みを取り出している。
彼女はクローゼットにほうきをしまっている。
郵便物が投入口に仕分けられているところである
クリップボードが一列に並べて掛けられている。

Part 2

2.	W	What if we move the seminar to a smaller conference room?	セミナーをもう少し小さい会議室に移してはどうですか。
	W	(A) My new phone number.	私の新しい電話番号です。
		(B) It was very informative.	とても参考になりました。
		(C) A lot of people have already signed up.	大勢の方がすでに申し込んでいます。
3.	W	I heard that Naomi has been given a promotion.	Naomi が昇進したそうですね。
	M	(A) She certainly deserves it.	彼女はまさにそれに値しますよ。
		(B) That's my office over there.	あそこが私の執務室です。
		(C) The application is due next week.	申請は来週が締め切りです。
4.	M	Why can't I connect my computer to this projector?	なぜ私のパソコンはこのプロジェクターに接続できないのですか。
	W	(A) I think the project's going well.	プロジェクトはうまくいっていると思います。
		(B) Because you need an adapter.	アダプターが必要だからです。
		(C) Fine, I'll be there soon.	大丈夫です、もうすぐそちらに着きます。
5.	M	Would you like me to print out the meeting agenda?	私が会議の議題を印刷しましょうか。
	W	(A) Simone already sent copies to everyone.	Simone がもう全員に送ってくれました。
		(B) No, in Room 405.	いいえ、405 号室にあります。
		(C) The conference center.	協議会場です。
6.	W	When are the interior decorators arriving?	内装業者はいつ到着するのですか。
	M	(A) It's on the top floor.	最上階にあります。
		(B) Maybe there's a lot of traffic.	もしかすると道路が混んでいるのかもしれません。
		(C) Yes, this dress is lovely.	はい、このドレスはすてきです。
7.	M	Let's discuss updating the Web site when you have time.	お時間があるときにウェブサイトの更新について話し合いましょう。
	W	(A) Have you registered yet?	もう登録しましたか。
		(B) Almost two o'clock.	もうすぐ 2 時です。
		(C) We can meet after lunch.	昼食の後に会えますよ。

Part 3

091

Questions 8 through 10 refer to the following conversation.

問題 8-10 は次の会話に関するものです。

W　Excuse me, I recently purchased this camera here, but I'm concerned because when I take photos of anything far away, they come out blurry.

すみません、最近こちらでこのカメラを購入したのですが、遠くにあるものを撮るとぼやけてしまうので、気になっています。

M　Well, it's difficult to take a sharp shot of something in the distance unless you have a camera stand. We have a few models here.

そうですね、カメラスタンドがないと遠くのものを鮮明に撮影するのは難しいものです。当店に数種類ございますよ。

W　Do you have any that are especially lightweight? I travel for work a lot. That's important to me because I have a lot of other equipment.

特に軽量のものはありますか。私は仕事で移動が多いんです。他にもたくさん機材があるので、私にはその点が重要です。

M　Well, the lightest tripod I know of is made by Miluco. I can have it sent here, but when will you need it by? I'll have to place a special order.

なるほど、私の知る限り最軽量の三脚は Miluco 製です。こちらにお取り寄せすることができますが、いつまでにご入り用ですか。特別な注文をしないといけませんので。

W　There's no rush.

急ぎませんよ。

8. 女性はどんな問題について男性に相談していますか。

(A) カメラのバッテリーが充電されない。
(B) メモリーカードの容量がいっぱいである。
(C) キャリーケースの大きさが足りない。
(D) 画像が鮮明でない。

9. 女性はどんな特徴が重要だと言っていますか。

(A) 色
(B) 使いやすさ
(C) 耐久性
(D) 重さ

10. 男性は "I'll have to place a special order" という発言で、何を示唆していますか。

(A) 女性は別の商品を選んだ方がいい。
(B) 女性はオンラインで依頼を出す必要があるだろう。
(C) 商品がすぐには入手できないかもしれない。
(D) 店長の手助けが必要である。

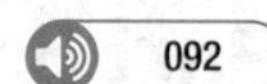

Questions 11 through 13 refer to the following conversation and schedule.

問題 11-13 は次の会話と予定表に関するものです。

M Hey, Julie. Have you finished the advertisement for the Westover Hotels? They're coming in next Friday to see the final version for their advertising campaign.

やあ、Julie。Westover ホテルの広告は完成しましたか。次の金曜日に先方が広告キャンペーンの完成版を見に来社されることになっています。

W Actually, I'm just adding a couple of finishing touches to the ad. The revised version should be ready by tomorrow afternoon.

実は、ちょうど広告に最後の仕上げを幾つか追加しているところなんです。修正版は明日の午後までには準備できるはずです。

M OK. Just let me know when you're done.

分かりました。完了したら私に知らせてください。

W Sure thing. Hey, do you remember what time we're meeting with them on Friday?

もちろんです。あの、金曜日は何時に先方と会うのか覚えていますか。

M No, I don't remember, but I know it's in Conference Room 215. You can check the schedule on our Web site.

いいえ、覚えていませんが、215 会議室なのは確かです。予定表をうちのウェブサイトで確認できますよ。

予定表

時間	会議室	クライアント
8:30	109	Wheaton グループ
9:30	215	Westover ホテル
10:30	330	Bedichek 提携会社
11:30	262	Abidi 医療社

11. 話し手たちはどの業界で働いていると思われますか。

(A) 銀行
(B) 広告
(C) 科学技術
(D) 接客

12. 女性は明日の午後までに何をする予定ですか。

(A) 荷物を発送する
(B) 発売日を確認する
(C) 修正を終える
(D) 顧客の意見を検討する

13. 図を見てください。会合はいつ行われますか。

(A) 8:30
(B) 9:30
(C) 10:30
(D) 11:30

Part 4

093

Questions 14 through 16 refer to the following tour information.

問題 14-16 は次のツアー情報に関するものです。

 W I want to welcome you all to this tour of the historic Schmidt Mansion, designed by renowned architect Gerhard Schmidt. This tour will cover just the mansion itself and will last approximately one hour. Now, we'll take a close look at the unique features of the exterior of the house. When we get outside, you'll notice the grounds are also quite remarkable and contain many notable sculptures. Don't forget, admission to the Schmidt Mansion includes unguided access to the grounds.

有名な建築家 Gerhard Schmidt によって設計された由緒ある Schmidt 邸のこの見学ツアーに、皆さまを歓迎いたします。このツアーは邸宅のみをご案内するもので、所要時間は約 1 時間です。さて、家屋外観の独特な特徴を近くで見てみましょう。屋外に出ますと、庭園もまた大変素晴らしく、多数の注目すべき彫刻があることにお気付きになるでしょう。Schmidt 邸の入場料にはガイドなしの庭園見学も含まれていますので、どうぞお忘れなく。

14. Gerhard Schmidt とは誰ですか。

(A) 俳優
(B) 建築家
(C) 芸術家
(D) 歴史家

15. 聞き手たちはツアーで何をしますか。

(A) バス旅行に行く
(B) 邸宅について学ぶ
(C) お土産を買う
(D) 歴史的な文書を読む

16. 話し手はなぜ "admission to the Schmidt Mansion includes unguided access to the grounds" と言っていますか。

(A) 聞き手たちに庭園の散策を勧めるため
(B) 聞き手たちにツアー料金の変更を知らせるため
(C) もっと多くのツアーガイドの必要性を強調するため
(D) 庭園の音声ガイダンスを宣伝するため

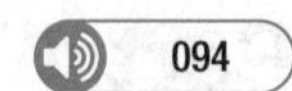

Questions 17 through 19 refer to the following announcement.

問題 17-19 は次のお知らせに関するものです。

W I'd like to tell you about a change we decided to make. We're transitioning from small shampoo bottles to large, wall-mounted shampoo dispensers in each of our guest rooms. Guests may ask you why we made this change. I'd suggest that you emphasize our company's commitment to reducing plastic waste. Most will appreciate our pledge to protect the environment. But if anyone complains, please encourage them to fill out a comment card at the front desk. Upper management would really like some feedback on this change.

決定した変更点について皆さんにお伝えしたいと思います。当ホテルでは、各客室で、小さなシャンプー容器から壁据え付け式の大型シャンプーディスペンサーに移行します。お客さま方は、なぜこのような変更を行ったのかと皆さんにお尋ねになるかもしれません。プラスチックごみ削減に向けた当社の取り組みを強調するとよいでしょう。ほとんどの方は環境を守るという当ホテルの誓いを評価してくださると思います。しかし、もしどなたかが苦情を訴えるようなら、フロントにあるご意見カードへのご記入を勧めてください。経営陣は今回の変更に関する感想がぜひとも欲しいだろうと思います。

17. 話し手はどこで働いていると思われますか。

(A) ヘアサロン
(B) ホテル
(C) 国立公園
(D) 空港

18. 話し手は何について話していますか。

(A) オンライン広告
(B) 営業時間の延長
(C) インターンの採用
(D) 容器の変更

19. 聞き手たちは顧客に何をすることを勧めるべきですか。

(A) ご意見カードに記入する
(B) 予約をする
(C) 会報を申し込む
(D) 職に応募する

Section 16 正解／スクリプト／訳

正解一覧

Part 1	1 (D)					
Part 2	2 (C)	3 (B)	4 (A)	5 (C)	6 (A)	7 (B)
Part 3	8 (B)	9 (C)	10 (D)	11 (C)	12 (B)	13 (A)
Part 4	14 (C)	15 (D)	16 (A)	17 (A)	18 (C)	19 (D)

Part 1

095

1. Look at the picture marked number 1 in your test book.
問題用紙の 1 の写真を見てください。

M
(A) Some shopping bags are being loaded into a car.
買い物袋が車に積まれているところである。

(B) Some cars have stopped at a traffic light.
車が信号で停車している。

(C) A woman is driving a car into a parking garage.
女性が屋内駐車場に車を乗り入れている。

(D) A woman is getting into a car.
女性が車に乗ろうとしている。

Part 2

2\. M Can you include a graphic on this presentation slide?
このプレゼンテーションのスライドに画像を入れることはできますか。

W (A) She gave an informative presentation.
彼女は有益なプレゼンテーションを行いました。

(B) No, near the graphic design department.
いいえ、グラフィックデザイン部の近くです。

(C) Sure, that should be easy to do.
もちろん、簡単にできるはずです。

3\. M When are we putting up the new window display?
新しいウィンドウディスプレイはいつ飾るのですか。

M (A) To promote some new products.
新商品を売り込むためです。

(B) This weekend, I think.
今週末だと思います。

(C) No, I didn't see them.
いいえ、それらを見かけませんでした。

4\. M Why is the store out of wireless headphones?
なぜこの店ではワイヤレスヘッドフォンが品切れなのですか。

W (A) There was a special offer.
特価販売があったのです。

(B) We close at seven.
当店は7時に閉店いたします。

(C) A few members of the team.
チームのうちの数人です。

5\. W When will the textile delivery arrive?
布地の配送はいつ届きますか。

M (A) The return address.
差出人住所です。

(B) Take a left at the corner.
その角で左折してください。

(C) Let me call the supplier.
供給業者に電話してみます。

6\. W I'm interested in buying the blue sofa from this page of the catalog.
カタログのこのページにある青いソファを買おうかと思っています。

M (A) Oh, that's from last season's edition.
ああ、そちらは昨シーズン版に掲載されているものです。

(B) The pile over there.
あちらの山です。

(C) Print the poster in color, please.
ポスターはカラーで印刷してください。

7\. W Can you recommend a place for us to have dinner near the hotel?
ホテルの近くで夕食を取れる良い店を教えてもらえませんか。

M (A) Your bill comes to 21 dollars.
お会計は21ドルになります。

(B) Most restaurants have already closed.
ほとんどのレストランがもう閉まっています。

(C) It's my favorite recipe.
私のお気に入りのレシピです。

Part 3

097

Questions 8 through 10 refer to the following conversation with three speakers.

問題 8-10 は 3 人の話し手による次の会話に関するものです。

W1 Hello, Mr. Aziz. I'm Sunita.

こんにちは、Aziz さん。Sunita です。

M Nice to meet you.

はじめまして。

W1 We're so glad your consultancy will be helping us. We've had some issues with last year's refrigerator and air conditioner models, and they've had a negative impact on our company's reputation.

御社のようなコンサルタント会社がお力添えくださることになって大変ありがたいです。昨年の冷蔵庫とエアコンの機種に問題があって、弊社の評判に悪影響をもたらしているものですから。

M That's why I'm here. I'll provide you with a strategy to repair your corporate image by more effectively responding to some of that bad press you've been getting.

そのために私はこちらに伺ったわけです。御社が被っている悪評にもっと効果的に対処することで企業イメージを回復する戦略を私がご提供します。

W1 That's great. I'd like to introduce you to Ms. Diaz, our vice president of marketing.

素晴らしい。あなたに Diaz さんをご紹介しますね。弊社のマーケティング本部長です。

W2 Hello, Mr. Aziz. We can start by reviewing our marketing plan for the new products. I've put together a presentation for you in the conference room. Shall we?

こんにちは、Aziz さん。新製品のマーケティングプランの見直しから始めましょう。あなたのために会議室にプレゼンテーションをまとめてあります。始めましょうか。

M Thank you, Ms. Diaz.

ありがとうございます、Diaz さん。

8. 女性たちはどこで働いていると思われますか。

(A) 保険会社
(B) 電化製品製造会社
(C) 旅行代理店
(D) 会計事務所

9. 男性はなぜ雇われたのですか。

(A) 求人キャンペーンを監督するため
(B) オフィス機器を修理するため
(C) 企業イメージを改善するため
(D) 顧客感謝イベントを企画するため

10. Diaz さんは何を準備していますか。

(A) 販促用パンフレット
(B) 取扱説明書
(C) 従業員名簿
(D) プレゼンテーション

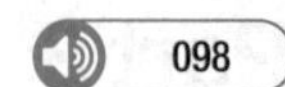

Questions 11 through 13 refer to the following conversation and company logos.

問題11-13は次の会話と会社ロゴに関するものです。

W Good morning, Gerhard. What's on my schedule today?

おはようございます、Gerhard。今日の私の予定はどうなっていますか。

M Hi, Ms. Watanabe. You have a meeting with the sales director at ten, and a client luncheon at noon.

おはようございます、Watanabeさん。10時に営業部長との会議、正午に顧客と昼食会です。

W Great. Thanks!

了解です。ありがとう！

M Oh, and your morning meeting has been moved to the third-floor conference room. The maintenance crew is repairing the ventilation system on the first floor.

あっ、それから朝の会合は3階の会議室に変更になりました。保守作業班が1階の換気システムを修理しているのです。

W OK. Any updates from the marketing department about our new logo design?

分かりました。当社の新しいロゴデザインのことでマーケティング部から最新情報はありましたか。

M Yes — they just sent over these options.

はい——ちょうどこちらの候補を送ってきました。

W Hmm... I don't like the diamond. My favorite is the one with the company's full name.

うーん…ひし形のものは好きではないですね。私が一番好きなのは社名が全表記で入っているロゴです。

M With the "W" in the circle? I like that one, too.

丸の中にWが入ったものですか。私もそれが好きです。

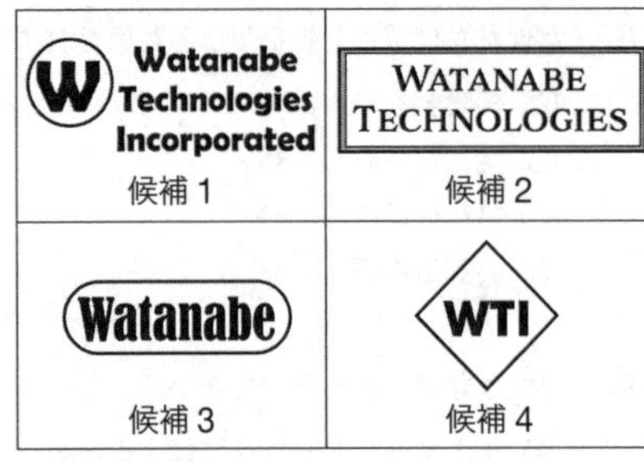

11. 男性は誰だと思われますか。

(A) グラフィックデザイナー
(B) 社長
(C) 重役補佐
(D) コンピューター技術者

12. 会合の場所はなぜ変更になったのですか。

(A) プレゼンテーション用のスクリーンが必要だから
(B) 保守作業が行われているから
(C) もっと広い部屋が要請されたから
(D) レストランが昼食を提供していないから

13. 図を見てください。女性はどのロゴの候補を最も気に入っていますか。

(A) 候補1
(B) 候補2
(C) 候補3
(D) 候補4

Part 4

099

Questions 14 through 16 refer to the following telephone message.

問題 14-16 は次の電話のメッセージに関するものです。

W Hello, Ms. Thompson, this is Eun-Hee Kim from Weston-Albright Accountants. As you know, we're looking for someone with expertise in tax law, and we were very impressed by your experience in that area. We'd like you to come in for an interview next week. Our vice president will be on-site, and she'd like to meet you. My assistant will call you to set up a time that's convenient. And we'll arrange for a car to meet you at the train station and bring you to our office.

もしもし、Thompson さん、Weston-Albright 会計事務所の Eun-Hee Kim です。ご承知の通り、私たちは税法に関する専門知識をお持ちの方を探しておりまして、その分野でのあなたのご経験に大変感銘を受けました。来週、面接にお越しいただきたく存じます。当事務所の副所長も同席する予定で、あなたにお会いするのを楽しみにしております。私のアシスタントがお電話を差し上げて、ご都合の良い日時を設定するようにいたします。また、車を手配してあなたを駅までお迎えにあがり、当事務所までご案内いたします。

14. 話し手によると、聞き手の資質について何が素晴らしいですか。

(A) 外国語能力
(B) 専門分野の著書
(C) 税法に関する知識
(D) 上級学位

15. 話し手は、聞き手に誰と会ってほしいと思っていますか。

(A) 見込み客
(B) 研究部長
(C) 人材コンサルタント
(D) 副所長

16. 話し手は何を手配すると言っていますか。

(A) 車での送迎
(B) 製品の配達
(C) 昼食会議
(D) 写真撮影会

100

Questions 17 through 19 refer to the following excerpt from a meeting and graph.

M Today, I'll be presenting on the results of the promotional event we held last quarter. As you recall, this promotion was held to create interest in our latest collection of winter clothes. We hoped that this would increase sales. If you look at the graph, you'll notice that clothing sales actually went down during the month we had the event and remained steady after that. Since this is not the outcome we expected, I think we should e-mail a questionnaire to some of our customers. Hopefully we can figure out what caused this drop in sales.

問題 17-19 は次の会議の一部とグラフに関するものです。

本日は、前四半期に実施した販促イベントの結果について報告します。ご記憶の通り、この販促活動は冬物衣料の最新コレクションへの関心を引き起こすために実施されました。私たちはこれが売り上げを伸ばしてくれることを期待したわけです。グラフをご覧になれば、実際には衣料の売り上げはイベントを実施した月に下がり、その後もそのままであることがお分かりいただけるでしょう。これは私たちが期待した結果ではありませんので、お客さまの一部にEメールでアンケートを取るべきだと思います。うまくいけば、何がこの売り上げの低下をもたらしたのかを突き止められるでしょう。

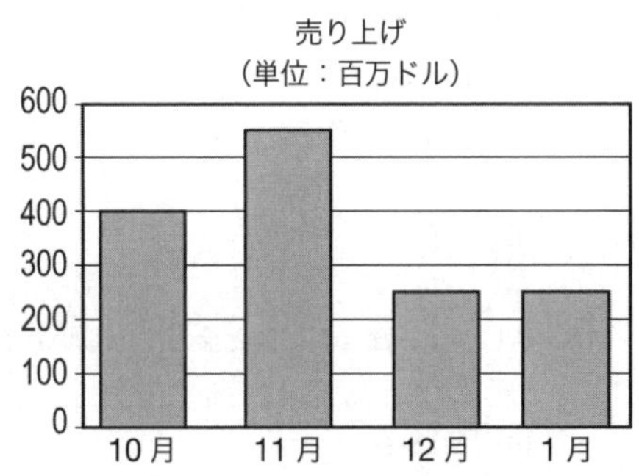

17. この会社は何を売っていますか。

(A) 衣料
(B) 電子機器
(C) 美容製品
(D) スポーツ用具

18. 図を見てください。どの月に会社は販促イベントを実施しましたか。

(A) 10月
(B) 11月
(C) 12月
(D) 1月

19. 話し手は何を提案していますか。

(A) 割引を提供すること
(B) テレビCMを制作すること
(C) 製品を検査すること
(D) 顧客の意見調査をすること

Section 17 正解／スクリプト／訳

正解一覧

Part 1	**1** (A)					
Part 2	**2** (A)	**3** (C)	**4** (A)	**5** (B)	**6** (C)	**7** (A)
Part 3	**8** (B)	**9** (D)	**10** (C)	**11** (D)	**12** (C)	**13** (A)
Part 4	**14** (A)	**15** (D)	**16** (B)	**17** (D)	**18** (A)	**19** (B)

Part 1

1. Look at the picture marked number 1 in your test book.
問題用紙の 1 の写真を見てください。

W
(A) A bucket has been placed under the counter.
カウンターの下にバケツが置かれている。

(B) One of the people is weighing some vegetables.
人々のうちの 1 人が野菜の重さを量っている。

(C) One of the people is turning on a stove.
人々のうちの 1 人がこんろに火をつけている。

(D) A plate has been filled with food.
皿が食べ物でいっぱいである。

Part 2

2. W When should I come back for my next checkup?
次の検診には、いつ来ればいいですか。

M (A) In six months.
6カ月後に。
(B) As long as they can.
彼らが可能な限りは。
(C) I'll return it tomorrow.
明日それをお返しします。

3. W Do you think our customers will like our new logo?
顧客は当社の新しいロゴを気に入ると思いますか。

M (A) We're going to the park this afternoon.
私たちは今日の午後、公園に行きます。
(B) Customer service is open now.
カスタマーサービスは今営業しています。
(C) Yes, it's very attractive.
はい、とても魅力的ですから。

4. W Which company won the contract?
どの会社が契約を勝ち取りましたか。

M (A) Those negotiations are ongoing.
その交渉は継続中です。
(B) The winning score was two to one.
勝利スコアは2対1でした。
(C) Replacing outdated computer systems.
古くなったコンピューターシステムの入れ替えです。

5. M Does the train always stop operating so early?
電車はいつもこんなに早く運行を終了するのですか。

W (A) No, the following Monday.
いいえ、次の月曜日です。
(B) There's construction work on track nine.
9番線で工事があるのです。
(C) This watch is very old.
この時計はとても古いです。

6. M The new manager is really effective, isn't she?
新しい部長は本当に有能ですよね?

W (A) A time management seminar.
時間管理に関するセミナーです。
(B) It had great special effects.
素晴らしい特殊効果が使われていました。
(C) Well, she did come from the Smith Corporation.
まあ、彼女はSmith社から来ましたからね。

7. M How do I get reimbursed for travel expenses?
交通費はどのように払い戻しを受けるのですか。

W (A) Did you keep your receipts?
領収書を取ってありますか。
(B) That is very expensive.
それはとても高額です。
(C) I agree completely.
まったく同感です。

Part 3

103

Questions 8 through 10 refer to the following conversation.

問題 8-10 は次の会話に関するものです。

M Hi, Mariam. It's Hao Nan. I'm calling because I want to take some potential international clients out to dinner when I meet with them in Dallas on Friday. I've never been there.

もしもし、Mariam。Hao Nan です。お電話しているのは、外国からの見込み客の方々と金曜日にダラスで会う際、夕食にお連れしたいと思っているためです。私はそこに行ったことがないものですから。

W Well, whenever I'm there, I take people to the Metropolitan Restaurant, because they have a large menu. Lots of variety.

そうですね、私はダラスに行くといつも皆さんを Metropolitan レストランに連れて行きます。メニューが豊富なので。本当にいろいろありますよ。

M They're really important executives. We need to impress them, because we've been trying to get them to upgrade their factories with our newest welding machines. I'm hoping they'll make a decision in our favor soon.

先方はとても重要な地位にある役員の方々です。私たちは好印象を与えなければなりません。なにしろ、当社の最新の溶接機で先方の工場の性能を高めてもらおうと私たちはずっと頑張ってきたわけですから。近々、先方がこちらの望み通りの決断をしてくれることを願っています。

W Hmm, you should get in touch with Vladimir — he grew up in Dallas. He'll have some better ideas.

ふーむ、あなたは Vladimir に連絡した方がいいと思いますよ――彼はダラス育ちです。彼にはもっといい案があるでしょう。

8. 男性はなぜ "I've never been there" と言っていますか。

(A) 誤解を正すため
(B) お薦めを尋ねるため
(C) 驚きを表すため
(D) 申し出を受け入れるため

9. 男性は、見込み客たちがどんな決断をすることを願っていますか。

(A) 研究資金を提供する
(B) ダラスでの滞在を延長する
(C) 工場を見学する
(D) 機械設備を購入する

10. なぜ女性は Vladimir に連絡することを提案していますか。

(A) 彼は顧客と親しい。
(B) 彼は熟練のシェフである。
(C) 彼はダラス出身である。
(D) 彼は予定の融通が利く。

104

Questions 11 through 13 refer to the following conversation and pie chart.

問題 11-13 は次の会話と円グラフに関するものです。

W Kentaro, I wanted to talk to you about the budget for the salon. I've reviewed our expenses for the last few months, and I'm concerned about how much we pay for utilities.

Kentaro、サロンの予算について話したいと思っていました。この数カ月の支出を見直したところ、光熱費の支払額が気になっています。

M Hmm. What do you think we can do?

うーん。何ができると思いますか。

W We could reduce the cost of utilities by changing the type of lights we use in the salon and asking the stylists to unplug their chargers for hair clippers when not in use.

サロンで使う照明の種類を変えたり、使っていないときはバリカン充電器のプラグを抜くようにスタイリストたちに頼んだりすることで、光熱費のコストを抑えられるかもしれません。

M You know, maybe the extra money could go toward making new promotional materials.

ほら、浮いたお金は新しい販促物を作るのに回してもいいかもしれないですね。

W Good idea.

いい考えですね。

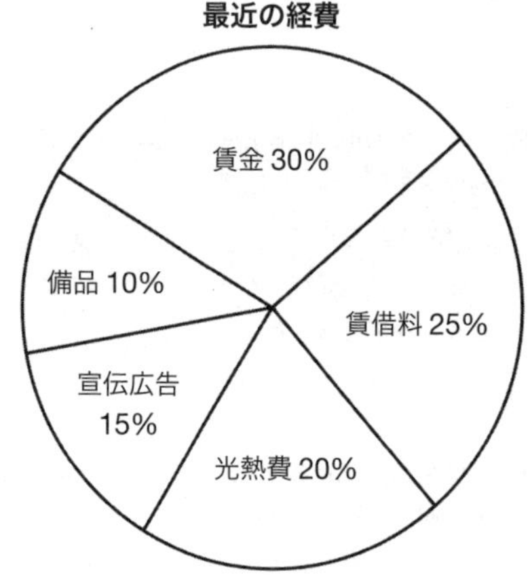

11. 話し手たちはどんな種類の事業を所有していると思われますか。

(A) 食料品店
(B) 電器店
(C) 歯科医院
(D) ヘアサロン

12. 図を見てください。女性は予算のどの割合を気にしていますか。

(A) 30 パーセント
(B) 25 パーセント
(C) 20 パーセント
(D) 15 パーセント

13. 男性は浮いたお金を何に使うことを提案していますか。

(A) 販促物を作ること
(B) 研修会の予定を立てること
(C) 新しい設備を購入すること
(D) 追加の従業員を雇うこと

Part 4

105

Questions 14 through 16 refer to the following introduction.

問題 14-16 は次の紹介に関するものです。

M Welcome to the annual conference on airport management. Today's keynote speaker is Martina Vogel, who is one of the nation's top property consultants. She'll be talking about how she established healthy dining options in the Westerville International Airport. Ms. Vogel was hired by that airport because so many visitors complained about the unhealthy menu items in the airport restaurants. While waiting for their flights, passengers were unhappy because there weren't enough meals that included fresh fruits and vegetables. In her speech, Ms. Vogel will explain how she encouraged health-food restaurants to lease retail space at the airport. Now, please welcome Martina Vogel.

空港運営の年次会議にようこそ。本日の基調講演者はMartina Vogel、国内トップの不動産コンサルタントのお一人です。Vogelさんには、健康的な飲食店という選択肢をどのようにしてWesterville国際空港に定着させたのかをお話しいただきます。Vogelさんが同空港に雇われたのは、非常に多くの利用客が空港レストランの不健康なメニューについて苦情を訴えていたからです。フライトを待つ間、新鮮な果物や野菜を含む食事が少ないせいで搭乗客は不満に思っていました。講演では、Vogelさんがどのようにして健康食レストランに空港の店舗スペースを借りるよう働きかけたのかを詳しくお話しいただきます。それでは、Martina Vogelさんをお迎えしましょう。

14. 聞き手たちはどんな種類のイベントに参加していますか。

(A) 業界会議
(B) オープン記念行事
(C) 研修会
(D) 取締役会

15. Martina Vogelとは誰ですか。

(A) 医師
(B) 報道記者
(C) 航空会社パイロット
(D) ビジネスコンサルタント

16. 話し手によると、なぜMartina Vogelは雇われましたか。

(A) モバイルアプリを設計するため
(B) 顧客の苦情に対処するため
(C) 政府による規制を監督するため
(D) 一般の認識を高めるため

106

Questions 17 through 19 refer to the following talk and floor plan.

W Hello, new interns! I'm Geeta Harris, head of the Human Resources Department here at Hansen Pharmaceuticals. We're very happy to have the five of you working with us this summer. I'll start the day by getting you all set up in the shared office space you'll be working in. I'm sure you'll love your office — it's conveniently located next to the stairs and across from the break room. Oh, and... after lunch you'll go to the security desk to get your pictures taken for your employee badges.

問題 17-19 は次の話と見取り図に関するものです。

こんにちは、新しいインターンの皆さん！私は Geeta Harris、当 Hansen 製薬会社の人事部長です。この夏、5人の皆さんが私たちと一緒に働いてくださることをとてもうれしく思っています。今日はまず、皆さんが働くことになる共用オフィスでもろもろの準備をしていただきます。皆さんはきっとオフィスを気に入ると思いますよ——階段の隣で休憩室の向かいという便利な場所にありますから。あっ、それから…昼食の後、皆さんは社員証用の写真を撮ってもらうために保安デスクに行くことになっています。

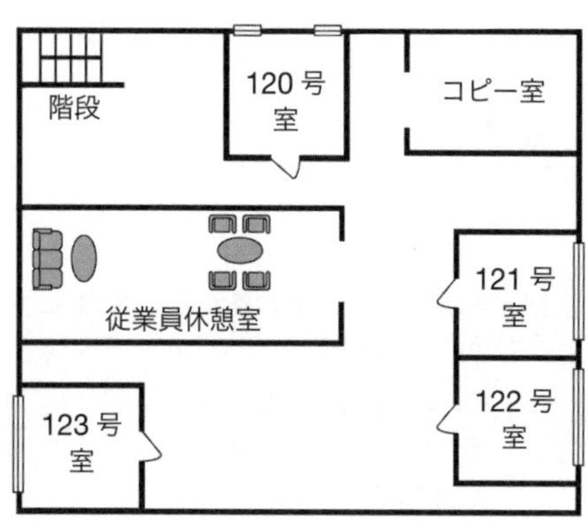

17. 聞き手たちは誰ですか。

(A) 保守作業員
(B) 就職希望者
(C) 訪問中の顧客
(D) 会社のインターン

18. 図を見てください。話し手はどのオフィスについて言及していますか。

(A) 120 号室
(B) 121 号室
(C) 122 号室
(D) 123 号室

19. 聞き手たちは昼食の後、どこに行きますか。

(A) コンピューター室
(B) 保安デスク
(C) 講堂
(D) 屋外の中庭

Section 18 正解／スクリプト／訳

正解一覧

Part 1	1 (A)					
Part 2	2 (C)	3 (C)	4 (A)	5 (B)	6 (C)	7 (B)
Part 3	8 (D)	9 (A)	10 (B)	11 (B)	12 (A)	13 (B)
Part 4	14 (B)	15 (A)	16 (B)	17 (D)	18 (C)	19 (B)

Part 1

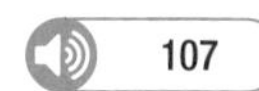

1. Look at the picture marked number 1 in your test book.
問題用紙の 1 の写真を見てください。

W (A) A shelf has been installed near the ceiling.
棚が天井の近くに取り付けてある。

(B) Some boxes are being unloaded from a vehicle.
箱が車から降ろされているところである。

(C) She's pushing a door closed.
彼女はドアを押して閉めている。

(D) She's rolling a bin up a ramp.
彼女は大型のごみ箱を転がしながら斜面を上がっている。

Part 2

2. M Is he taking the eight o'clock train or a later one?
彼は8時の電車に乗りますか、それとももっと遅い電車ですか。

M (A) It's two blocks farther.
それは2ブロック先です。
(B) He usually does.
彼はたいていそうします。
(C) I think it's a later one.
遅い電車だと思います。

3. W Did the maintenance staff already clean the windows?
保守作業員はもう窓を清掃しましたか。

M (A) Would you like any?
少しいかがですか。
(B) In the file cabinet.
書類棚の中です。
(C) No, they'll do it today.
いいえ、今日それを行います。

4. M Could we have our next client dinner at the Italian restaurant?
次の顧客とのディナーはあのイタリア料理店にしませんか。

W (A) OK, we'll go there next time.
分かりました、次回はそこに行きましょう。
(B) No thanks, I'm not hungry.
結構です、お腹は空いていません。
(C) Please follow me to your table.
お席までご案内いたします。

5. W How much does an express ticket cost?
急行券は幾らですか。

M (A) Oh, I've been there before.
ああ、私は以前そこへ行ったことがあります。
(B) It's the same as regular service.
普通列車と同じです。
(C) About twenty minutes.
約20分です。

6. M The weekly brainstorming session is at noon today, right?
毎週定例のブレスト会議は今日の正午ですよね?

W (A) The stop sign at the intersection.
交差点の一時停止標識です。
(B) No, after you.
いえ、あなたからどうぞ。
(C) The team leader is out on vacation.
チームリーダーが休暇で不在なのです。

7. M Why didn't they hire the same architect?
なぜ彼らは同じ建築士を雇わなかったのですか。

W (A) Yes, I have the blueprints.
はい、私は設計図を持っています。
(B) Didn't you get the e-mail?
あなたはEメールを受け取らなかったのですか。
(C) The new building will be done next year.
その新しい建物は来年完成予定です。

Part 3

109

Questions 8 through 10 refer to the following conversation with three speakers.

問題8-10は3人の話し手による次の会話に関するものです。

W1 Hi, Chan-Ho and Min Wang. Do you have time to help me prepare for our end-of-the-season warehouse sale?

お疲れさま、Chan-Ho、Min Wang。シーズン末の倉庫セールの準備を手伝ってくれる時間はありますか。

M Sure. What needs to be done?

もちろんです。何をする必要がありますか。

W1 Well, here's a list of items that will be sold at a discount. Before you put them on the clearance racks, scan their bar codes to make sure that they are in fact discounted items.

ええと、これが値引きで販売される商品のリストです。処分品の棚に陳列する前に、バーコードをスキャンして実際に値引き商品であることを確認してください。

W2 Great. I have the bar code scanner, so I can start checking the merchandise now.

よかった。ここにバーコードスキャナーがあるので、私はすぐに商品チェックを始められます。

W1 Right. Thanks, Min Wang. And Chan-Ho, let's clear out the pallets at the front of the warehouse. We'll need that space for the clearance racks.

そうですね。ありがとう、Min Wang。それではChan-Ho、倉庫の前にあるパレットを片付けましょう。処分品の棚用にそのスペースが必要になりますから。

M Sure. Just let me find the key for the forklift, and I'll meet you over there.

分かりました。私はまずはフォークリフトの鍵を探すので、向こうで落ち合いましょう。

8. 話し手たちは何の準備をしていますか。

(A) 取締役会
(B) 年次点検
(C) 配送品の到着
(D) 販売イベント

9. Min Wangは何をしますか。

(A) バーコードをチェックする
(B) 掲示物を貼る
(C) 請求書を印刷する
(D) 時間を確認する

10. 男性は何を探す必要がありますか。

(A) 看板
(B) 鍵
(C) 軍手
(D) 記入用紙

110

Questions 11 through 13 refer to the following conversation and e-mail inbox.

問題 11-13 は次の会話と E メールの受信トレイに関するものです。

W Good morning, Mr. Zhang. Did you receive the meeting invitations I sent this morning?

おはようございます、Zhang さん。今朝私がお送りした会議の招集通知を受け取っておられますか。

M Hi, Helen. No, I've just sat down at my computer. The traffic this morning was terrible.

おはよう、Helen。いいえ、ちょうどコンピューターの前に座ったところです。今朝の交通渋滞はひどかったもので。

W Oh, no problem. So, I sent out four staff-meeting invitations for next month, but then I realized that August twenty-fourth is the day of our company picnic. Should we have the meeting on a different day that week?

あら、大丈夫です。それで、来月の 4 つのスタッフ会議の招集通知をお送りしたのですが、その後で 8 月 24 日は社内ピクニックの日だと気付きました。その週の別の日にその会議を設定した方がいいですか。

M No, let's just cancel it. Everyone's schedule is so full at this time of year. It's nearly impossible to find a time when the whole team is free.

いや、中止にしましょう。一年のこの時期は、みんな予定がぎっしり詰まっています。チーム全員が空いている時間を見つけるのはほぼ不可能ですから。

Eメール 受信トレイ

Davis, Helen 売り上げ最新報告	8 月 24 日
Davis, Helen 予算審査	8 月 17 日
Davis, Helen プロジェクト立案	8 月 10 日
Davis, Helen スタッフ配置の決定	8 月 3 日

11. なぜ男性は今朝、まだ E メールを見ていないのですか。

(A) 今まで休暇を取っていた。
(B) オフィスに遅く到着した。
(C) 彼のコンピューターが修理中である。
(D) 彼のインターネットサービスが機能していない。

12. 図を見てください。どの会議が中止になりますか。

(A) 売り上げ最新報告会議
(B) 予算審査会議
(C) プロジェクト立案会議
(D) スタッフ配置の決定会議

13. 男性は同僚たちについて何と言っていますか。

(A) 助けになってくれている。
(B) とても忙しい。
(C) ピクニックを楽しみにしている。
(D) 講習会に出席する予定である。

Part 4

111

Questions 14 through 16 refer to the following telephone message.

W Hello, this is Keisha Phillips with Cunningham Acting Troupe. I'm calling because we're looking for a new venue for our upcoming performance of *Sunflowers for Louis*. Unfortunately, the theater we rented for this performance has just been sold to a real estate developer and is no longer available. I've done some preliminary looking online for spaces that we could rent on a short-term basis. Your performing arts center could be just what we're looking for. I was especially interested in the option to use your technical staff, instead of providing our own. Anyway, I was hoping to schedule a tour of the center today. Please call me back at 555-0165. Thanks so much.

問題 14-16 は次の電話のメッセージに関するものです。

もしもし、Cunningham 劇団の Keisha Phillips と申します。当劇団の次回作『ルイにひまわりを』を上演する新しい会場を探しているため、お電話しています。不運なことに、この公演のために当劇団が借りた劇場は、つい先日不動産開発業者に売却されてしまい、もう使えません。私は短期で借りられそうなスペースをとりあえずインターネットで探してみました。そちらの舞台芸術センターは、まさに私たちが探しているようなものかもしれません。特に、自分たちでスタッフを用意する代わりに、そちらの技術スタッフをお借りできるプランがいいと思いました。とにかく、今日センターを見学する予定を決められたらと思っておりました。555-0165 まで折り返しお電話をください。よろしくお願いいたします。

14. 話し手はどんなイベントについて言及していますか。

(A) 授賞式
(B) 劇場公演
(C) 記者会見
(D) 展示会

15. 話し手は芸術センターについて何が気に入っていると言っていますか。

(A) 技術サポート
(B) 定期送迎サービス
(C) 夏季割引
(D) 広々とした部屋

16. 話し手は何を依頼していますか。

(A) 費用見積もり
(B) 建物の見学
(C) 情報が掲載された小冊子
(D) ケータリングのお薦め

112

Questions 17 through 19 refer to the following excerpt from a meeting and calendar.

M As you know, today's meeting is to finalize the themes for the coming months for our business magazine. Now, I put together a calendar with the article topics you suggested at our last meeting. Social media was the most popular topic on that list, but remember, many other magazines have published articles about that. So, let's brainstorm ideas for another theme. Once we finish this calendar, our next step will be to interview business leaders in the community. I think we should talk to two or three experts for each topic.

問題 17-19 は次の会議の一部と予定表に関するものです。

ご承知の通り、本日の会議はうちのビジネス誌の今後数カ月のテーマを最終決定するためのものです。さて、前回の会議で皆さんが提案してくれた記事のトピックを予定表にまとめました。ソーシャルメディアがそのリストで最も人気のあるトピックでしたが、いいですか、他の多くの雑誌がそれに関する記事を掲載しています。そこで、別のテーマについてアイデアを出し合いましょう。この予定表を仕上げたら、次のステップは地域のビジネスリーダーたちへの取材です。各トピックについて、2名ないし3名の専門家に話を聞いた方がいいと思います。

予定表

1月	2月
テーマ： 新興企業	テーマ： 統率力
3月	**4月**
テーマ： ソーシャルメディア	テーマ： 中小企業

17. 話し手はどこで働いていると思われますか。

(A) ビジネススクール
(B) 地域の公民館
(C) 人材紹介会社
(D) 雑誌出版社

18. 図を見てください。どの月のテーマが変更になりますか。

(A) 1月
(B) 2月
(C) 3月
(D) 4月

19. 話し手によると、次のステップは何ですか。

(A) 広告主に連絡すること
(B) ビジネスの専門家に取材すること
(C) 職責を割り当てること
(D) ウェブサイトに情報を掲載すること

Section 19 正解／スクリプト／訳

正解一覧

Part 1	1 (D)					
Part 2	2 (C)	3 (A)	4 (C)	5 (A)	6 (B)	7 (B)
Part 3	8 (A)	9 (B)	10 (C)	11 (B)	12 (C)	13 (D)
Part 4	14 (B)	15 (A)	16 (C)	17 (A)	18 (A)	19 (C)

Part 1

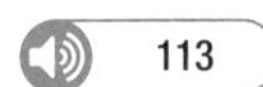

1. Look at the picture marked number 1 in your test book.
問題用紙の 1 の写真を見てください。

M
(A) A brick wall is being painted.
レンガの壁にペンキが塗られているところである。

(B) A fence is being repaired.
フェンスが修理されているところである。

(C) A railing has been installed next to some stairs.
手すりが階段の横に設置されている。

(D) A construction vehicle has been parked near a building.
工事車両が建物の近くに止められている。

Part 2

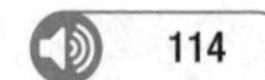

2. M Do you think we'll need extra chairs?
追加の椅子が必要になると思いますか。

W (A) I'm happy to read the announcements.
私が喜んで発表を読み上げますよ。
(B) The new board chair.
新しい役員会会長です。
(C) Actually, I think we have enough.
実のところ、十分な数があると思いますよ。

3. W Who led the management meeting today?
今日は誰が経営会議を主導しましたか。

M (A) Emiko did.
Emiko がしました。
(B) It'll take about a week.
1 週間ほどかかるでしょう。
(C) A recorded greeting.
録音されたあいさつです。

4. W Isn't there a free shuttle service to the conference?
会議場までの無料送迎サービスはないのですか。

M (A) She isn't leaving until next week.
彼女は来週まで出発しません。
(B) Three presentations this morning.
今朝の 3 つのプレゼンテーションです。
(C) Our hotel is just across the street.
当ホテルはちょうど通りを挟んで向かい側でございます。

5. M We'll need materials for the new project, won't we?
新しいプロジェクトに資材が必要になりますよね?

W (A) They're ready to be picked up.
いつでも持っていける状態ですよ。
(B) Lunch is on the table.
昼食がテーブルに用意できています。
(C) Keep going straight.
ずっと真っすぐに進んでください。

6. W What days will you be in the office next week?
あなたは来週、何曜日にオフィスにいる予定ですか。

M (A) It looks like a balloon.
それは風船のように見えます。
(B) I'm going to Singapore to meet some clients.
私は顧客に会いにシンガポールに行く予定なのです。
(C) Usually on the tenth floor of the building.
普段はビルの 10 階です。

7. W Would you like sugar or cream in your tea?
紅茶に砂糖かクリームをお入れになりますか。

M (A) She collects teaspoons.
彼女はティースプーンを集めています。
(B) I'll have both, please.
両方ともお願いします。
(C) We missed the deadline.
私たちは締め切りに間に合いませんでした。

Part 3

Questions 8 through 10 refer to the following conversation with three speakers.

問題8-10は3人の話し手による次の会話に関するものです。

W Hi, Carlos and Anil. I need your opinion — it's about customer feedback on our latest line of T-shirts.

お疲れさま、Carlos、Anil。あなたたちの意見が聞きたいのです――当社の最新のTシャツシリーズに対するお客さまの反応についてです。

M1 Sure, what is it?

いいですよ、どんなことですか。

W Well, customers have been complaining. They say the tags at the neckline in the back of the shirts are uncomfortable.

実は、お客さまからずっと苦情が来ています。Tシャツの裏側の襟ぐりに付いているタグが当たって着心地が悪いというんです。

M2 Hmm… There are some shirts where the tag information is printed on the fabric itself. We can see if our T-shirt vendor can supply us with those, right Carlos?

うーん…。タグの内容が生地自体にプリントされているシャツもありますよ。当社のTシャツの仕入先がそういったシャツを供給可能かどうか確かめられますよね、Carlos?

M1 That's true. But I'm worried that change may increase our budget. Let's look into the cost difference first before making a decision.

その通りです。ただ、その変更で予算が増えるかもしれないのが心配です。決断を下す前にまずは費用の差を調べてみましょう。

8. 話し手たちはどこで働いていると思われますか。

(A) 衣料品会社
(B) ソフトウエア会社
(C) 運送会社
(D) 出版社

9. 女性はどんな問題について言及していますか。

(A) 退職する従業員がいる。
(B) 苦情を言っている顧客がいる。
(C) 閉鎖になる倉庫がある。
(D) 停止中のコンピューターサーバーがある。

10. Carlosは何を調べることを提案していますか。

(A) 融資を受けられる可能性
(B) デザインの人気度
(C) 変更にかかる費用
(D) 立地の利点

116

Questions 11 through 13 refer to the following conversation and mobile phone application.

問題 11-13 は次の会話と携帯電話アプリに関するものです。

M I'm glad we attended this year's publishing trade show. The writers' panel was really interesting.

今年の出版展示会に参加してよかったです。作家の公開討論会が本当に興味深かったですね。

W Yes, there were so many good books, it'll be hard to decide which ones to purchase for our library.

ええ、良い本がすごくたくさんあって、私たちの図書館用にどの本を購入するか決めるのに苦労しそうですね。

M That's true! Oh — we should probably head to the airport soon. Our flight's in three hours.

本当ですね！ おっと——たぶんすぐに空港に向かったほうがいいですよ。私たちの乗る便は 3 時間後です。

W Hm… I'm really hungry. How about we grab a quick snack? It'd be better than airport food.

うーん…。私はすごくお腹が空いています。さっと軽く食べませんか。空港の食事よりおいしいと思いますよ。

M Good idea.

いい考えですね。

W I have this helpful application on my smartphone. See? It locates taxis nearby. You click on the closest one and just wait to be picked up.

私のスマートフォンにこんな便利なアプリが入っています。ほらね。近くのタクシーを見つけてくれるんです。一番近いタクシーをクリックして、あとは迎えが来るのを待つだけです。

M Nice! Two minutes might be too soon. Let's request the taxi that's ten minutes away.

いいですね！ 2 分だと早過ぎるかもしれません。10 分離れているタクシーを呼びましょう。

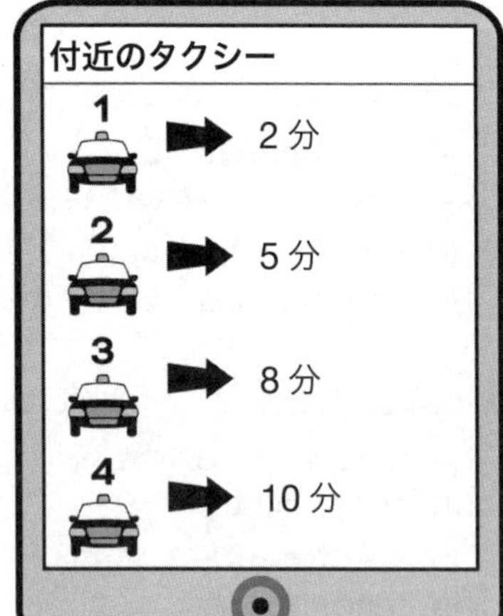

11. 話し手たちはどんなイベントに参加しましたか。

(A) 就職説明会
(B) 出版展示会
(C) 退職祝いのパーティー
(D) 美術館の開館式

12. 女性は何をしたいと言っていますか。

(A) ニュース記事を読む
(B) 書店を訪れる
(C) 食べ物を購入する
(D) 航空便を予約する

13. 図を見てください。話し手たちはどのタクシーを呼びますか。

(A) タクシー 1
(B) タクシー 2
(C) タクシー 3
(D) タクシー 4

Part 4

117

Questions 14 through 16 refer to the following broadcast.

問題 14-16 は次の放送に関するものです。

W Hi. I'm Fatima Khan with tonight's business report. According to a recent study, traffic congestion has steadily increased over the past few years. This congestion is causing the trucking industry to lose thousands of dollars each year. The lost revenue comes mostly from frequent refueling of vehicles that have to sit in traffic for hours. As a result, trucking companies are considering upgrading their vehicles to more energy-efficient models. Talks are currently under way between Dynamic Motors and the National Trucking Association to arrive at a deal.

こんにちは。Fatima Khan が今夜のビジネスレポートをお届けします。最近の研究によると、交通渋滞がここ数年で着実に増加しています。こうした渋滞によって、トラック運送業界は毎年数千ドルの損失を被っています。この減収は主として、何時間も渋滞で動けない車両への頻繁な燃料補給から生じています。その結果、トラック運送各社は車両をよりエネルギー効率のよい上位車種に変更することを検討しています。現在、Dynamic モーターズ社と全国トラック運送協会との間で契約締結に向けた話し合いが行われています。

14. 最近の研究は何を示しましたか。

(A) より多くの商取引がオンラインで行われている。
(B) 交通渋滞が増えている。
(C) 従業員はフレックスタイム制で働く方を好む。
(D) オフィス機器は定期的にアップグレードされるべきである。

15. 話し手によると、業界はどんな問題を抱えていますか。

(A) 収益の損失
(B) 製造の遅れ
(C) 製品の品質低下
(D) 有能な従業員の不足

16. 話し手によると、どのような変更が検討されていますか。

(A) 新しい場所に移転すること
(B) 会社のウェブサイトを更新すること
(C) よりエネルギー効率のよい車種を使うこと
(D) 従業員の在宅勤務を認めること

118

Questions 17 through 19 refer to the following excerpt from a meeting and contact list.

M Let's start today's Human Resources department meeting with an update about the employee wellness program. Last week we launched a program to promote physical activity and a healthy lifestyle for our employees. Interested participants will join a team, and they'll log their exercise hours to win monthly prizes. The only team that still has open spots is the Yellow team. So, if employees ask you which team they can join, direct them to that contact person.

問題 17-19 は次の会議の一部と連絡先一覧に関するものです。

本日の人事部会議は、社員の健康プログラムに関する最新情報から始めましょう。先週、当社社員の運動と健康的ライフスタイルを促進するプログラムを開始しました。興味のある参加者は 1 つのチームに所属し、毎月の賞品獲得を目指して運動時間を記録します。まだ空きがある唯一のチームはイエローチームです。ですから、社員がどのチームに入れるかを尋ねてきたら、そこの担当者の所に行かせてください。

担当者	チーム
Wei Zhou	ブルー
Aisha Osman	グリーン
Rita Lopez	イエロー
Kavi Krishnan	オレンジ

17. 話し手はどんな部署で働いていますか。

(A) 人事
(B) 情報技術
(C) 給与支払い業務
(D) 施設管理

18. 話し手は何について話していますか。

(A) 健康プログラム
(B) 事前説明会の日程
(C) 全社会議
(D) 販売コンテスト

19. 図を見てください。話し手は、社員は誰に連絡するべきだと言っていますか。

(A) Wei Zhou
(B) Aisha Osman
(C) Rita Lopez
(D) Kavi Krishnan

Section 20 正解／スクリプト／訳

正解一覧

Part 1	1 (A)					
Part 2	2 (C)	3 (B)	4 (B)	5 (C)	6 (A)	7 (A)
Part 3	8 (B)	9 (A)	10 (C)	11 (A)	12 (C)	13 (D)
Part 4	14 (D)	15 (C)	16 (B)	17 (C)	18 (D)	19 (B)

Part 1

1. Look at the picture marked number 1 in your test book.
問題用紙の 1 の写真を見てください。

M (A) There's a patterned carpet covering the floor.
柄物のカーペットが床を覆っている。

(B) Some pictures have been taken out of their frames.
数枚の絵が額縁から取り外されている。

(C) Some chairs are stacked in the corner.
幾つかの椅子が隅に積み重ねられている。

(D) There's a vase of flowers displayed on the table.
花瓶がテーブルの上に飾られている。

Part 2

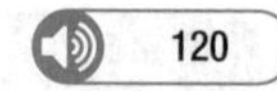

2. M Would you like tea or coffee with your dessert?
デザートとご一緒に紅茶かコーヒーはいかがですか。

M (A) The table by the window.
窓際のテーブルです。
(B) Just a few more ingredients.
あと幾つかの材料だけです。
(C) I'll have some tea.
紅茶をください。

3. W Wasn't Mr. Yamada at the party yesterday?
Yamada さんは昨日、パーティーに出なかったのですか。

M (A) A large hotel venue.
ホテルの広い会場です。
(B) No, he was sick.
出ませんでした、体調が悪かったのです。
(C) From five to seven tomorrow.
明日の 5 時から 7 時です。

4. M How can I get a doctor's appointment today?
どうすれば今日、医者の診察予約が取れますか。

W (A) I'm very grateful to you.
あなたにとても感謝しています。
(B) The clinic on Allen Street is rarely busy.
Allen 通りの診療所なら、めったに混んでいませんよ。
(C) Last Tuesday at three.
先週の火曜日の 3 時です。

5. M Who expressed interest in your book manuscript?
どこがあなたの本の原稿に興味を示しましたか。

W (A) At the end of August.
8 月の終わりです。
(B) Just a grapefruit for me.
私はグレープフルーツ 1 個だけで結構です。
(C) A couple of academic publishers.
2、3 の学術系出版社です。

6. M Why was the product launch delayed?
製品発売はなぜ遅れたのですか。

W (A) We haven't made changes to the schedule.
私たちはスケジュールに変更を加えていませんよ。
(B) Actually, lunch is in the conference room.
実のところ、昼食は会議室になります。
(C) By the loading dock.
荷物搬入口のそばです。

7. W Are you driving to the agricultural fair this weekend?
今週末の農産物品評会には車で行きますか。

M (A) Parking there is expensive.
あそこの駐車料金は高いのです。
(B) He's with the farmers' association.
彼は農業組合に加入しています。
(C) I think that price is fair.
その価格は適正だと思います。

Part 3

121

Questions 8 through 10 refer to the following conversation.

問題 8-10 は次の会話に関するものです。

M Welcome to the show *Our Hometown Music Scene* on WQZ radio. I'm your host, Alexi Mayer. Today we're reporting live from the big rock-and-roll concert at Central Arena. Our reporter, Anna Kim, is standing outside the ticket office. Anna, how does it look over there?

WQZ ラジオの番組『わが町の音楽シーン』へようこそ。ホストの Alexi Mayer です。今日はセントラルアリーナでの大規模なロックコンサートから生中継でお届けします。番組レポーターの Anna Kim がチケット売り場の外に立っています。Anna、そちらの様子はどうですか。

W Well, Alexi, people have been in line for hours. As you know, the band has been at the top of the music charts for the past seven months.

はい、Alexi、皆さんもう何時間も並んでいます。ご存じの通り、バンドはこの 7 カ月間、音楽チャートの首位に輝いています。

M Yes. And their latest album sold over eleven million copies. I'm here inside the arena with the lead singer. I'll be interviewing her about the band's tour right after this short commercial break.

そうなんです。そして彼らの最新アルバムは 1,100 万枚以上を売り上げました。私はリードボーカルと一緒に、このアリーナの中にいます。短いコマーシャルの後すぐに、バンドのツアーについて彼女にインタビューします。

8. 話し手たちは何について話していますか。

(A) 就職説明会
(B) 音楽コンサート
(C) 季節限定セール
(D) スポーツイベント

9. 女性は "people have been in line for hours" という発言で、何を意味していますか。

(A) イベントがとても人気がある。
(B) 追加の働き手が必要である。
(C) 軽食はもう購入できない。
(D) 情報を受け取るのに長い時間がかかっている。

10. 男性は次に何をしますか。

(A) 掲示物を貼る
(B) チラシを配る
(C) インタビューを行う
(D) 写真を撮る

Questions 11 through 13 refer to the following conversation and table.

問題 11-13 は次の会話と表に関するものです。

W I was surprised at the amount of feedback we received about the new space adventures video game — from the game testers I mean.

新しい宇宙冒険ビデオゲームについて寄せられた反響の多さに驚きました——ゲームテスターたちからの、という意味です。

M I hope they liked the sound effects. We worked so hard on those.

音響効果を気に入ってもらえたのであればいいですね。それに関して私たちはかなり頑張りましたから。

W Everybody commented on how good the sound is. But the graphics in the desert race section need some work — the image was jumpy when players tried to race at high speeds.

皆さん、音響がどんなに素晴らしいかをコメントしていましたよ。ただ、砂漠レース・セクションのグラフィックにもう少し工夫が必要ですね——プレーヤーが高速で走ろうとすると、映像がこま落ちしていました。

M Hmm. I'll start working on that one today — try to figure out what the problem is.

うーん。私は今日からその点に取り組みますよ——何が問題なのかを突き止めようと思います。

W Good. I've got a meeting with the marketing team later. We still haven't decided on a name for this game, but they've narrowed it down to five possibilities.

よかった。私はこの後、マーケティングチームと打ち合わせがあります。このゲームの名前がまだ決まっていませんが、彼らは5つの候補まで絞り込んでいます。

レベル 1	新世界
レベル 2	アトランティス探検
レベル 3	ビッグボスの挑戦
レベル 4	砂漠レース
レベル 5	最終決戦

11. 女性は何に驚きましたか。

(A) 使用者たちからの反響の量
(B) 製品売り上げの伸び
(C) グラフィックデザインの新たな手法
(D) 商品化契約に関する問題

12. 図を見てください。男性はどのレベルに取り組むと言っていますか。

(A) レベル 2
(B) レベル 3
(C) レベル 4
(D) レベル 5

13. 何が後でマーケティングチームと話し合われますか。

(A) 宣伝ポスター
(B) チームの割り当て業務
(C) 納期
(D) 商品名

Part 4

123

Questions 14 through 16 refer to the following excerpt from a meeting.

問題 14-16 は次の会議の一部に関するものです。

W Thank you for inviting me to speak at today's meeting of the city transportation board. I'm Emiko Sato, the lead engineer for the high-speed train project. I'm happy to announce that phase one of the project is nearing completion — high-speed trains are now serving riders throughout many areas of the city. And, while it's true that I was the one who oversaw phase one, I'd like to emphasize that several people were on the team. Adriana Diaz made this work a priority from day one, and Hasan Rashad was always available on call. Next, as the city moves into phase two of the project, stations will be renovated to enhance the customer experience.

市交通局の本日の会議で話をするようお招きいただき、ありがとうございます。高速鉄道プロジェクト主任技術者の Emiko Sato と申します。プロジェクトの第 1 段階が完了間近であるとお知らせできることをうれしく思います——高速鉄道は現在、市のさまざまな地区で乗客を乗せて運行しています。そして、確かに私が第 1 段階を監督しましたが、チームには何人かの仲間がいたことを強調したいと思います。Adriana Diaz はプロジェクト初日からこの仕事を優先してくれましたし、Hasan Rashad はいつでも呼び出しに対応してくれました。次に、市はプロジェクトの第 2 段階に進み、お客さまの利用体験を向上させるべく駅の改修が行われます。

14. 話し手は誰ですか。

(A) 報道記者
(B) 環境活動家
(C) 電車の車掌
(D) 交通技術者

15. 話し手はなぜ "several people were on the team" と言っていますか。

(A) 過失の責任を否定するため
(B) 新しい納期の要求を拒否するため
(C) 他の貢献者をたたえるため
(D) 将来に向けた新戦略を提案するため

16. 話し手はプロジェクトの第 2 段階で何が行われると言っていますか。

(A) 新たな決済システムが導入される。
(B) 駅が改修される。
(C) 追加の作業員が雇われる。
(D) 追加の輸送ルートが開設される。

124

Questions 17 through 19 refer to the following telephone message and floor plan.

W Hey, Soo-Min, it's your roommate, Isabel ! I went to see that apartment we saw listed… the one over on South Street. I think it's a great option! It's much closer to downtown than our current apartment, which is just too far away. Three of the bedrooms are in the back, so you and our other roommates can take those. And since I can sleep through traffic noise, I'll take the one facing South Street. I think we should go for it. The realtor said we'll need to provide a security deposit by this Friday… you know, in case anything gets damaged. It's just one month's rent, though. Anyway, let me know what you think!

問題 17-19 は次の電話のメッセージと間取り図に関するものです。

もしもし、Soo-Min、ルームメイトの Isabel です！掲載されているのを見た例のアパートを見に行ってきました…South 通りにあるアパートです。とてもいい物件だと思いますよ！今のアパートより繁華街にはるかに近いんです、今のはちょっと遠過ぎますから。寝室のうち 3 つは奥にあるので、あなたと他のルームメイトたちがそこを使えばいいと思います。そして私は車の騒音の中でも眠れるので、South 通りに面した部屋を使います。私たちはここに決めるべきだと思います。不動産屋さんは、今週金曜日までに保証金を払う必要があると言っていました…ほら、万が一何かを損傷した場合のためです。といっても、家賃 1 カ月分だけです。とにかく、あなたの意見を聞かせてください！

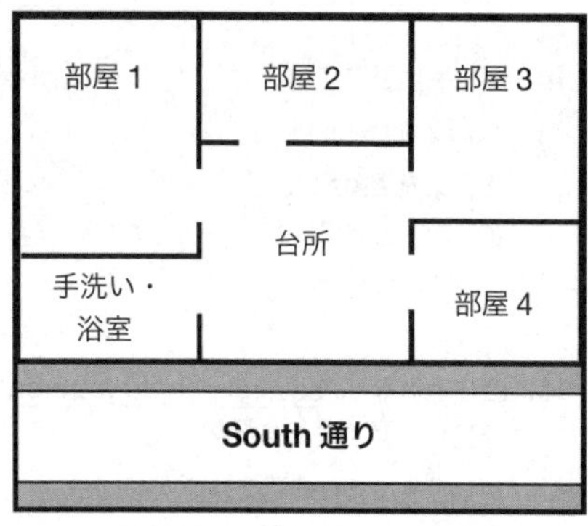

17. なぜ話し手は今のアパートに不満なのですか。

(A) 狭い。
(B) 家賃が高い。
(C) 繁華街から遠い。
(D) 補修が必要である。

18. 図を見てください。話し手はどの部屋を使うと申し出ていますか。

(A) 部屋 1
(B) 部屋 2
(C) 部屋 3
(D) 部屋 4

19. 話し手によると、金曜日までに何が提出される必要がありますか。

(A) 連絡先を記入したフォーム
(B) 保証金
(C) 推薦状
(D) 在職証明書

公式 TOEIC® Listening & Reading トレーニング 2
リスニング編
別冊 正解／スクリプト／訳

2023 年 12 月 6 日　第 1 版第 1 刷発行

著者	ETS
編集協力	株式会社 エディット 株式会社 群企画 株式会社 WIT HOUSE
表紙デザイン	山崎 聡
発行元	一般財団法人 国際ビジネスコミュニケーション協会 〒 100-0014 東京都千代田区永田町 2-14-2 山王グランドビル 電話　(03) 5521-5935
印刷・製本	日経印刷株式会社

Printed in Japan
ISBN 978-4-906033-72-0